MIDDLE
EASTERN
COOKBOOK

MIDDLE EASTERN COOKBOOK

MARIA KHALIFÉ

NEW HOLLAND

First published in 2006 by New Holland Publishers (UK) Ltd
London • Cape Town • Sydney • Auckland

Garfield House
86–88 Edgware Road
London W2 2EA
www.newhollandpublishers.com

80 McKenzie Street
Cape Town 8001
South Africa

Level 1, Unit 4
14 Aquatic Drive
Frenchs Forest, NSW 2086
Australia

218 Lake Road
Northcote
Auckland
New Zealand

1 3 5 7 9 10 8 6 4 2

ISBN 1 84537 407 X

Senior Editor: Corinne Masciocchi
Design: Sue Rose
Photography: Stuart West
Food styling: Stella Murphy
Editorial Direction: Rosemary Wilkinson
Production: Hazel Kirkman
Reproduction by Colourscan Overseas, Singapore
Printed and bound by Times Offset, Malaysia

TEMPERATURE CONVERSION CHART		
Celsius	Fahrenheit	Gas mark
120°	250°	½
140°	275°	1
150°	300°	2
160°	325°	3
180°	350°	4
190°	375°	5
200°	400°	6
220°	425°	7
230°	450°	8
240°	475°	9

CONTENTS

THE WIDE CULINARY REPERTOIRE and extensive knowledge of Middle-Eastern cuisine I possess stem from several sources. I am the editor of a culinary magazine, owner of a cookery school and producer of 'Soufra Daimeh', the TV cookery show broadcast both in the Middle East and internationally. During my wide-ranging travels across the Middle East, I explored a passion for cooking alongside local women to discover their culinary secrets, and, through this, improved my understanding of traditional cooking habits. I have translated my experiences into this book, which contains easy-to-follow methods to ensure that cooking these recipes is simple, enjoyable and exciting.

The hardest part of writing this book was choosing which recipes to include and which to leave out. Ultimately, I decided on a selection that is currently gaining more popularity in Western cultures. I wanted to make sure that while each recipe was simple to prepare, no ingredients were included which could not be easily obtained throughout the world.

Identifying the origin of an individual recipe can be difficult. Many of the finest dishes of Middle-Eastern heritage first emerged centuries ago, and this type of food was often spread by the paths of marching armies over the years, no doubt gaining or losing a herb or two along the way. The Ottoman Turks brought with them the thin filo pastry and the coffee now served throughout the Middle East, while other cultures and peoples also left their marks. The huge diversity includes spices from India, yoghurt from Russia, okra from Africa, tomatoes from the Moors of Spain and dumplings from the Mongol invaders. By now, claims as to the origins of a certain dish are varied and hard to prove. For instance, whereas one authority claims the Syrians obtained a certain dish from the Egyptians, another source is convinced it was brought to Egypt at a later date, stolen from the Turks!

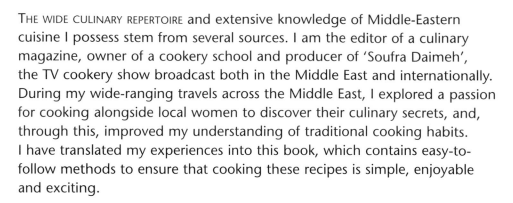

Equally important are the produce, traditions and religion of each country. There is a certain level of similarity between all Arab countries, increasing in strength between neighbours, such as the Lebanon, Syria and Jordan, or the states of the Gulf region, but each area has its unique culinary characteristics. So, when I attribute a certain dish to one country, it does not necessarily mean that it originated there, only that the given method of preparation is the customary one for that area.

The variety of dishes included in this book reflects the diversity of the Middle-Eastern region and the culture and hospitality of its people. Each recipe is given its traditional name alongside an English translation. Ingredients and terms which might be unfamiliar to you are explained in the Glossary (see pages 158–59) and, where appropriate, substitutes for some more unusual ingredients are given.

I have tried to create a balance between using the original preparation methods of the region to preserve the genuine flavours of each dish, and making the process simpler with the aid of conveniences such as a food processor, blender and meat grinder. If you have the luxury of these kitchen appliances, they will cut your preparation time and make your life a little easier without compromising the taste of the finished product.

Most of the ingredients used in this book will be familiar to the Western reader and are widely available in supermarkets. For others, though, you may have to search further afield in a Middle-Eastern food store.

I sincerely hope that you enjoy these recipes, and that this book may help to widen your knowledge and understanding of the rich Middle-Eastern culture through its varied cuisine.

Welcome to our table.

STARTERS

Starters, or mezza, are an important part of Middle-Eastern entertaining. It is always a social occasion when friends and family gather over a drink to nibble on appetizers and share the latest news before lunch or dinner. Starters may consist of three or four small dishes, but an elaborate array of tempting and mouthwatering appetizers is a more likely scenario. If you are looking to impress your guests, try the Parsley and cracked wheat salad (page 10), which is always received with pleasure. For an appetizer and a dip, try the Chickpeas and tahini dip (page 21) or the Aubergine and tahini dip (page 13). These are delicious with barbecued meat or chicken. Starters such as Spinach pies (page 14), Cheese rolls (page 24), Meat pies (page 20) and Chicken pies (page 27) can all be prepared in advance and frozen.

LEBANON

SERVES 4–6

360 g / 12^1/2 oz (4 cups) parsley
30 g / 1 oz (^{1}/3 cup) fresh mint leaves
1 small onion, peeled and finely chopped
1 tsp salt
^{1}/4 tsp black pepper
4 Tbsp fine burghul (fine cracked wheat)
5 medium firm ripe tomatoes, seeded and
  finely chopped
125 ml / 4 fl oz (^{1}/2 cup) lemon juice
125 ml / 4 fl oz (^{1}/2 cup) olive oil
Leaves from 1 romaine lettuce heart,
  to garnish

Tabbouleh
Parsley and cracked wheat salad

1 Rinse the parsley and mint thoroughly, then drain in a strainer. In a small bowl, mix the chopped onion with the salt and black pepper and set aside.

2 Rinse the burghul and drain it in a fine strainer, then transfer it to a large bowl.

3 Remove and discard the thick stalks of parsley and chop it finely. Also chop the mint leaves finely. Add the parsley and mint to the bowl, then add in the tomatoes, seasoned onion, lemon juice, olive oil, and season again to taste if necessary.

4 Transfer to a serving dish and garnish with the lettuce heart leaves. Serve on its own or with grilled or barbecued meat, chicken or fish.

UNITED ARAB EMIRATES

SERVES 4–6

1 kg / 2 lb 3 oz chicken wings
1 tsp salt
^{1}/2 tsp white pepper
125 ml / 4 fl oz (^{1}/2 cup) vegetable oil
1 medium onion, peeled and chopped
2 garlic cloves, peeled and crushed
70 g / 2^1/2 oz (^{3}/4 cup) fresh coriander,
  finely chopped
60 ml / 2 fl oz (^{1}/4 cup) lemon juice

Jawaneh dajaj
Golden chicken wings

1 Rinse the chicken wings and drain. Rub with the salt and pepper.

2 Heat the vegetable oil in a frying pan. Add the chicken wings and fry until golden brown, then remove from the pan and set aside.

3 Add the onions to the frying pan and cook until tender. Add the garlic and coriander and fry for 3 minutes, stirring regularly.

4 Return the chicken wings to the frying pan and stir in the lemon juice. Simmer over a low heat for 5 minutes until most of the juice has evaporated. Serve warm.

Parsley and cracked wheat salad

LEBANON

SERVES 4

1 large aubergine
1 garlic clove, peeled
1 tsp salt
60 g / 2 oz tahini
2 Tbsp yoghurt
Juice of 1 lemon
2 sprigs parsley and
  2 Tbsp olive oil, to garnish

Baba ghanouge
Aubergine and tahini dip

1 Preheat the oven to 220° C / 425° F. Pierce the aubergine with a fork. Place it on a baking tray and bake or grill over a charcoal fire for about 30 minutes until soft, turning frequently. Cool under running water.

2 Peel off the skin and remove the stem. Mash the pulp to a purée using a potato masher or a fork.

3 In a small bowl, crush the garlic with the salt and add to the aubergine purée. Stir in the tahini and yoghurt. Gradually blend in the lemon juice, mixing well. Pour into small serving dishes and garnish with sprigs of parsley and olive oil.

 IRAN

SERVES 5–6

2 large aubergines
60 ml / 2 fl oz (¼ cup) lemon juice or
  sour grape juice
1 Tbsp pomegranate molasses
Pinch of salt
¼ tsp black pepper
1 tsp marjoram
½ tsp dried mint
2 medium onions, peeled and grated
4 medium tomatoes, peeled and diced

Naaz khaatoon
Aubergines in pomegranate juice

1 Preheat the oven to 220° C / 425° F. Pierce the aubergines with a fork. Place them on a baking tray and bake or grill over a charcoal fire for about 30 minutes until soft, turning frequently. Cool under running water.

2 Peel off the skin and remove the stems. Mash the pulp to a purée using a potato masher or a fork. Add the lemon juice, pomegranate molasses, salt and pepper.

3 Transfer the mixture to a pan and cook over low heat for about 10 minutes. Add the marjoram, dried mint and grated onions. Mix well and cook for a further 1 minute, then remove from the heat. Mix in the tomatoes and serve hot or cold.

Aubergine and tahini dip

LEBANON

MAKES 30–35 PIES

For the dough
1 1/2 tsp active dry yeast
1 tsp caster sugar
60 ml / 2 fl oz (1/4 cup) warm water
450 g / 1 lb (3 cups) plain flour
125 ml / 4 fl oz (1/2 cup) vegetable oil
1 tsp salt
125 ml / 4 fl oz (1/2 cup) milk
125 ml / 4 fl oz (1/2 cup) water

For the filling
1 kg / 2 lb 3 oz spinach, rinsed and chopped
2 medium onions, peeled and finely chopped
Pinch of salt
3 medium tomatoes, chopped
4 Tbsp olive oil
2 Tbsp lemon juice
Black pepper, to taste
3 Tbsp sumac

Fatayir bi sbanigh

Spinach pies

1 Start by making the dough. In a large bowl, dissolve the yeast and the sugar in the warm water. Stir in the flour, oil, salt and milk. Add the water gradually and knead for 5 to 6 minutes until the dough is smooth and elastic. Cover the bowl with a damp cloth and set aside in a warm place for at least 1 hour until the dough has doubled in size.

2 In the meantime, make the filling. Squeeze out the excess water from the spinach and place in a large bowl. Add in the onions, salt, tomatoes, olive oil, lemon juice, pepper and sumac and mix thoroughly.

3 Divide the dough into 3 equal pieces. Roll out each piece on a lightly floured surface to a 1/2-cm (1/4-in) thickness, then cut into 10-cm (4-in) circles. You should be able to cut about 10 circles from each piece of dough.

4 Preheat the oven to 200° C / 400° F. Place 1 tablespoon of filling in the centre of each circle and bring up the edges together at three points to form a triangle. Pinch the edges together to seal the pies.

5 Arrange the pies on lightly greased baking trays. If desired, brush the pies with vegetable oil or beaten egg to give a golden colour. Bake for 20 minutes until golden brown. Serve cold.

SYRIA

MAKES 22 PIES

For the dough
1 1/2 tsp active dry yeast
60 ml / 2 fl oz (1/4 cup) warm water
1 tsp caster sugar
450 g / 1 lb (3 cups) plain flour
125 ml / 4 fl oz (1/2 cup) vegetable oil
1 tsp salt
125 ml / 4 fl oz (1/2 cup) milk
125 ml / 4 fl oz (1/2 cup) water

For the filling
3 Tbsp vegetable oil
1 large onion, peeled and chopped
4 Tbsp pine nuts
400 g / 14 oz minced beef
Pinch of salt
1/4 tsp of each: black pepper, cinnamon
   and allspice
3 medium tomatoes, chopped
125 ml / 4 fl oz (1/2 cup) yoghurt
1 Tbsp white wine vinegar
2 Tbsp lemon juice

Lahm bil ajine
Meat pies

1 Start by making the dough. In a large bowl, dissolve the yeast in the warm water. Stir in the sugar, flour, vegetable oil, salt and milk. Add the water gradually and knead for 5 to 6 minutes until the dough is smooth and elastic. Cover the bowl with a damp cloth and set aside in a warm place for at least 1 hour until the dough has doubled in size.

2 In the meantime, make the filling. Heat the vegetable oil in a frying pan. Add the onion and pine nuts and cook until golden brown. Add the minced beef and cook for 5 minutes until all the liquid has evaporated and the beef is brown. Season with the salt and spices, then remove from heat and set aside to cool.

3 Add the tomatoes, yoghurt, vinegar and lemon juice to the meat. Mix well and set aside.

4 Preheat the oven to 200° C / 400° F. Divide the dough into 2 equal pieces. Roll out each piece on a lightly floured surface to a 1/2-cm (1/4-in) thickness. Cut into 10-cm (4-in) circles. You should be able to cut about 11 circles from each piece of dough.

5 Place 1 level tablespoon of filling in the centre of each circle and bring up the edges together at four points to form a square. Pinch the edges together to seal the pies.

6 Arrange the pies on lightly greased baking trays. Bake for 20 minutes until golden brown and serve immediately.

 LEBANON

Hummus bi tahini

Chickpeas and tahini dip

SERVES 4

420 g / 15 oz (1 ¹/2 cups) canned cooked
  chickpeas
1 garlic clove, peeled and crushed
180 ml / 6 fl oz (³/4 cup) water
4 Tbsp tahini
125 ml / 4 fl oz (¹/2 cup) lemon juice
Pinch of salt
Parsley sprigs, ¹/2 tsp paprika and
  2 Tbsp olive oil, to garnish

1 Reserve 1 teaspoon of chickpeas for the garnish. Using a food processor or blender, process or blend until smooth the remaining chickpeas with the garlic and 60 ml / 2 fl oz (¹/4 cup) of the water.

2 Dissolve the tahini in the remaining water and lemon juice, then blend with the chickpea mixture. The mixture should be thick and smooth. Season with salt.

3 Pour the mixture into small dishes and garnish with the reserved chickpeas, parsley sprigs, paprika and olive oil. Serve with pitta bread and/or barbecued meat or chicken.

SAUDI ARABIA

MAKES 35 PIES

For the dough
1¹/₂ tsp active dry yeast
60 ml / 2 fl oz (¹/₄ cup) warm water
450 g / 1 lb (3 cups) plain flour
2 eggs
1 tsp salt
125 ml / 4 fl oz (¹/₂ cup) vegetable oil
1 cup water

For the filling
1 kg / 2 lb 3 oz leeks, rinsed and chopped
2 large onions, peeled and chopped
2 chilli peppers, chopped (optional)
Pinch of salt
1 tsp black pepper
1 Tbsp corn oil

Samboosak bel-koorat

Leek pies

1 Start by making the dough. In a large bowl, dissolve the yeast in the warm water. Stir in the flour, eggs, salt and vegetable oil. Add the water gradually and knead for 5 to 6 minutes until the dough is smooth and elastic. Cover the bowl with a damp cloth and set aside in a warm place for at least 1 hour until the dough has doubled in size.

2 In the meantime, make the filling. Mix the leeks with the onions, chilli peppers, salt, pepper and corn oil.

3 Preheat the oven to 200° C / 400° F. Divide the dough into 3 equal pieces. Roll out each piece on a lightly floured surface into a large rectangle. Brush with a generous amount of corn oil and cut into 5-cm (2-in) strips. Place 10 strips on top of each other and cut into 2.5-cm (1-in) squares. Dip each dough square in flour, then roll out into 10-cm (4-in) squares.

4 Place 1 tablespoon of leek mixture in the centre of each square. Fold 1 cm (¹/₂ in) of each edge over the filling to form a square pie, so that part of the filling is still visible. Press the edges at each corner.

5 Arrange the pies on a lightly greased baking tray. Bake for 15 to 20 minutes until golden brown. Serve hot.

LEBANON

SERVES 5

For the salad
1 kg / 2 lb 3 oz potatoes
60 ml / 2 fl oz (1/4 cup) olive oil
Salt, to taste
1/4 tsp black pepper
1 red pepper, diced
1 green pepper, diced
4 spring onions with tops, cut into thin pieces
3 garlic cloves, peeled and crushed
3 Tbsp parsley, finely chopped
Juice of 1 lemon

1 cucumber, sliced into rings, few mint leaves
  and pinch of sumac (optional), to garnish

Salatit al batata
Mashed potato salad

1 Rinse the potatoes. Cook them in salted water until tender, for about 20 to 25 minutes, then drain and peel them.

2 In a large bowl, mash the potatoes to a purée. Stir in the olive oil, salt and pepper. Add the red and green peppers, spring onions, garlic, parsley and lemon juice, and mix thoroughly.

3 Place the potato salad in a serving dish and smooth out the surface with a fork. Garnish with cucumber slices arranged around the sides of the dish, a few mint leaves in the centre and sprinkle with sumac, if using.

 LEBANON

MAKES 6 PIES

For the dough
1 1/2 tsp active dry yeast
1 tsp caster sugar
60 ml / 2 fl oz (1/4 cup) warm water
450 g / 1 lb (3 cups) plain flour
125 ml / 4 fl oz (1/2 cup) vegetable oil
1 tsp salt
1 Tbsp dry milk
240 ml / 8 fl oz (1 cup) water

For the topping
45 g / 1 1/2 oz (1/2 cup) dried thyme mix
  (see page 159)
125 ml / 4 fl oz (1/2 cup) olive oil

Mankoush
Thyme pies

1 Start by making the dough. In a large bowl, dissolve the yeast and sugar in the warm water. Stir in the flour, vegetable oil, salt and dry milk. Add the water gradually and knead for 5 to 6 minutes until the dough is smooth and elastic. Cover the bowl with a damp cloth and set aside in a warm place for at least 1 hour until the dough has doubled in size.

2 Preheat the oven to 200° C / 400° F. Divide the dough into 6 equal pieces. Roll out each piece on a lightly floured surface into 10-cm (4-in) circles. Flute the edges of each circle.

3 To make the topping, combine the dried thyme mix with the olive oil. Brush each circle with this mixture and prick with a fork to prevent swelling during baking. Place on a lightly greased baking tray or griddle and bake for 10 to 15 minutes. Serve hot.

EGYPT

SERVES 5–6

3 medium taroes
60 ml / 2 fl oz (1/4 cup) vegetable oil
2 medium onions, peeled and thinly sliced
2 Tbsp olive oil
1 litre / 35 fl oz (4 cups) water
250 g / 9 oz (1 cup) tahini
125 ml / 4 fl oz (1/2 cup) lemon juice
Pinch of salt
1/4 tsp white pepper
125 ml / 4 fl oz (1/2 cup) water
Chopped parsley, to garnish

Kalkas bi tahini
Taro with tahini

1 Peel the taroes, then rinse and cut them into medium-size cubes.

2 Heat the vegetable oil in a frying pan and add the taroes. Cook for about 10 minutes until light brown on all sides. Remove from the pan and drain on absorbent paper.

3 Brown the onions in the olive oil. Stir in the taro cubes and cover with the water. Bring to the boil, then reduce the heat. Simmer gently for 20 minutes until tender.

4 In a bowl, blend the tahini with the lemon juice, salt, pepper and water. Gradually add the liquid to the pan, stirring continuously. Reduce the heat and simmer gently for about 15 minutes until the sauce thickens. Serve cold. Garnish with chopped parsley.

 LEBANON

MAKES 24 ROLLS

350 g / 12 1/2 oz filo pastry
200 g / 7 oz grated halloumi cheese
200 g / 7 oz grated fetta cheese
100g / 3 1/2 oz gruyère cheese
4 Tbsp parsley, chopped
1 medium onion, peeled and finely chopped
2 eggs, beaten
240 ml / 8 fl oz (1 cup) vegetable oil

Rkakat bil jibm
Cheese rolls

1 If using frozen filo pastry, defrost thoroughly before use. Cut the pastry into twenty-four 12 x 15-cm (5 x 6-in) strips.

2 Mix together the three cheeses, parsley and onion. Place 2 tablespoons of the cheese mixture in the centre of the shorter side of each filo strip. Fold both left and right sides over the filling, then roll up firmly. Brush the end of the pastry with beaten egg to seal properly.

3 Deep fry the pies in hot vegetable oil for about 5 minutes, then drain on absorbent paper. Alternatively, arrange the rolls on a lightly greased oven tray, brush them with vegetable oil and bake in a preheated oven at 220° C / 425° F for 20 minutes until golden brown. Serve hot.

Taro with tahini

UNITED ARAB EMIRATES

MAKES 15 PIES

For the dough
1¹/₂ tsp active dry yeast
60 ml / 2 fl oz (¹/₄ cup) warm water
450 g / 1 lb (3 cups) plain flour
4 Tbsp rice flour or cornflour
1 tsp salt
3 Tbsp butter, melted
1 egg, beaten
190 ml / 6.5 fl oz (³/₄ cup) water

For the filling
3 Tbsp vegetable oil
90 g / 3 oz (1 cup) cabbage, chopped
90 g / 3 oz (1 cup) green beans, chopped
1 medium onion, peeled and finely chopped
1 green pepper, diced
2 garlic cloves, peeled and crushed
2 chicken breasts, boiled or grilled, and cut
   into small cubes
1 tsp white pepper
1 tsp salt

2 egg yolks, for brushing

Sambousik al dajaj
Chicken pies

1 Start by making the dough. In a large bowl, dissolve the yeast in the warm water. Stir in the flour, the rice or cornflour, salt, melted butter and beaten egg. Add the water gradually and knead for 5 to 6 minutes until the dough is smooth and elastic. Cover the bowl with a damp cloth and set aside in a warm place for at least 1 hour until the dough has doubled in size.

2 In the meantime, make the filling. Heat the vegetable oil in a pan. Stir-fry the cabbage, green beans, onion, green pepper and garlic until tender. Add the cooked chicken and season with white pepper and salt. Stir for a few minutes.

3 Preheat the oven to 200° C / 400° F. Divide the dough into 30 equal pieces. Roll out each piece on a lightly floured surface into 10-cm (4-in) circles.

4 Place a tablespoon of the filling in the centre of each circle. Brush the edges with egg yolk and cover each circle with another circle of dough. Pinch the edges together with a fork to seal. Brush the tops of each circle with egg yolk.

5 Bake for about 20 to 25 minutes until light brown. Arrange in a serving dish and serve hot.

SYRIA

SERVES 4–6

225g / 8 oz (1$^{1}/_{2}$ cups) fine burghul
  (fine cracked wheat)
500 g / 1 lb 2 oz lean minced lamb
Pinch of salt
1 small onion, peeled and grated
$^{1}/_{2}$ tsp black pepper
$^{1}/_{2}$ tsp allspice
1 tsp chilli paste
1 tsp paprika
$^{1}/_{2}$ tsp dried basil
$^{1}/_{2}$ tsp dried marjoram
3 Tbsp cold water
3 Tbsp mint leaves and
  2 Tbsp pine nuts, to garnish
Olive oil, to serve

Kibbeh nayye
Raw kibbeh

1 Rinse the burghul in cold water and leave to drain for 10 minutes.

2 Combine the burghul with the minced lamb, salt, onion, pepper, allspice, chilli paste, paprika, basil and marjoram. Moisten hands with a little cold water and knead the mixture well to a consistent paste, adding more cold water if necessary. Alternatively, use a food processor and process ingredients very quickly, adding 3 tablespoons cold water.

3 Place in a serving dish and flatten the surface with the back of a spoon. Garnish with the mint leaves and pine nuts and drizzle with olive oil.

 EGYPT

SERVES 4–6

1 kg / 2 lb 3 oz potatoes
240 ml / 8 fl oz (1 cup) vegetable oil,
  for frying
4 garlic cloves, peeled
1 tsp salt
90 g / 3 oz (1 cup) fresh coriander, chopped
$^{1}/_{2}$ tsp dried coriander
$^{1}/_{2}$ tsp ground red chilli
Juice of 1 lemon

Batatos bil kouzbara
Potatoes with coriander

1 Peel the potatoes, then rinse and cut them into small cubes. Re-rinse and drain.

2 Heat the vegetable oil in a large frying pan and add the cubed potatoes. Cook on a medium heat until golden brown, then drain on absorbent paper.

3 Crush the garlic with the salt and fry it with the fresh coriander in the pan in 2 tablespoons vegetable oil. Fry for 3 minutes until brown.

4 Stir in the potatoes, dried coriander, chilli and lemon juice. Simmer over a low heat for 2 to 3 minutes. Remove from the heat and serve hot.

Raw kibbeh

VEGETABLES AND GRAINS

Vegetables and grains constitute the main diet of most Middle-Eastern people. Aubergines, tomatoes, cracked wheat, broad beans, chickpeas, lentils and rice are just some of the produce of the land and the flavours of the cuisine.

Vegetables and grains are not only simple to prepare, but are nutritious and a rich source of protein. They are often served as main meals in the form of stews or soups, or ground into pastes, then made into patties. Alternatively, they can be mashed into purées or baked in the oven and served with bread, pickles or a salad. Their versatility means that they are delicious any time of the day.

LEBANON

SERVES 7

For the pumpkin mixture
1 kg / 2 lb 3 oz pumpkin, peeled and
  deseeded
2 medium onions, peeled and chopped
450 g / 1 lb (3 cups) fine burghul
  (fine cracked wheat)
75 g / 2^1/2 oz (^{1}/2 cup) plain flour
Pinch of salt
^{1}/4 tsp cinnamon
^{1}/4 tsp white pepper
4 Tbsp olive oil

For the stuffing
3 medium onions, peeled and chopped
2 Tbsp sumac
200 g / 7 oz (2 cups) Swiss chard, chopped
Salt, to taste
White pepper, to taste
^{1}/4 tsp cinnamon
Pinch of saffron
3 Tbsp olive oil
140 g / 5 oz (^{1}/2 cup) canned cooked
  chickpeas
60 g / 2 oz (^{1}/2 cup) walnuts, coarsely
  chopped

Kibbet yaktin
Pumpkin with cracked wheat

1 Start by making the pumpkin mixture. Remove the fibres from the pumpkin and dice into medium-size pieces. Place the pieces in a saucepan, cover with water and bring to the boil. Cook over a medium heat until tender, for about 25 minutes. Drain and set aside to cool.

2 When cool, squeeze out excess water from the pumpkin pieces. Place them in a food processor container with the onions and process to a purée.

3 Rinse the burghul and squeeze out the excess moisture. Add to the pumpkin with the flour, salt, cinnamon and pepper. Knead to amalgamate the ingredients.

4 To make the stuffing, rub the onions with sumac and place in a bowl. Add the Swiss chard, salt, pepper, cinnamon, saffron, olive oil, chickpeas and walnuts and mix well.

5 Preheat the oven to 220° C / 425° F. Grease a 30-cm (12-in) round oven-proof dish with olive oil. Knead the pumpkin mixture again until smooth and divide it into two equal portions. Place the first half in the bottom of the dish and press with your hands to form a smooth layer. Spread the stuffing evenly over this layer.

6 Divide the second half of the pumpkin mixture into five equal portions. Press each piece with your hands to form 2-cm (^{3}/4-in) thick shapes. Place the pieces over the stuffing and spread them evenly into a single layer to cover the stuffing completely. Brush the surface with olive oil, then make deep diagonal and horizontal cuts across the surface. Bake for 20 minutes. Serve cold.

LEBANON

SERVES 6

500 g / 1 lb 2 oz (2^1/$_2$ cups) long grain rice
1 tsp salt
100 ml / 3^1/$_2$ fl oz (^{1}/$_2$ scant cup) olive oil
2 large onions, peeled and chopped
500 g / 1 lb 2 oz green broad beans, shelled
1 litre / 35 fl oz (4 cups) water
Salt, to taste
^{1}/$_4$ tsp allspice
^{1}/$_4$ tsp black pepper

Foul akhdar bil rouz
Green broad beans with rice

1 Rinse the rice, then soak it in warm water with the salt for 45 minutes. Drain.

2 Heat the olive oil in a large saucepan and add the onions. Fry until light brown, then stir in the broad beans. Cook over a medium heat for about 5 minutes. Add the water and bring to the boil, then reduce the heat. Cover and simmer gently until tender, for about 15 minutes.

3 Add the rice to the saucepan and bring to the boil again, stirring once or twice, then reduce the heat. Cover and simmer gently until all the fluid has been absorbed and the rice is tender. Season with salt, allspice and pepper and remove from heat. Transfer to a serving dish and serve hot or cold.

 YEMEN

SERVES 4–6

2 Tbsp vegetable oil
2 large onions, peeled and finely chopped
2 garlic cloves, peeled and crushed
3 medium tomatoes, peeled and chopped
^{1}/$_2$ tsp of each: black pepper, cumin, cinnamon, cloves and cardamom
1 whole green chilli
1 Tbsp tomato paste
1250 ml / 2.6 pints (5 cups) water
1 chicken stock cube
200 g / 7 oz (1 cup) black eye beans
4 Tbsp fresh coriander, chopped

Loubia mjafafi
Black eye bean stew

1 Heat the vegetable oil in a large pan. Add the onions and garlic and fry for 4 to 5 minutes over a medium heat until golden brown.

2 Add the tomatoes, all the spices, the green chilli and tomato paste and cook over a medium heat for 3 to 4 minutes. Add the water, stock cube and black eye beans and bring to the boil. Simmer over a low heat for 40 minutes or until beans are cooked. Remove from the heat and add the coriander and season to taste. Serve with boiled rice.

Green broad beans with rice

SYRIA

SERVES 6

500 g / 1 lb 2 oz (2^1/$_2$ cups) dry chickpeas
^{3}/$_4$ tsp bicarbonate of soda
4 garlic cloves, peeled and crushed
1 tsp salt
1 Tbsp dried mint
1 Tbsp butter
1250 ml / 2.6 pints (5 cups) plain yoghurt
1^1/$_2$ pitta bread pockets, toasted and broken
  into small pieces
^{1}/$_4$ tsp paprika
4 Tbsp toasted pine nuts

Fattit al hommus
Chickpeas in yoghurt sauce

1 Soak the chickpeas in water and bicarbonate of soda overnight. The next day, thoroughly rinse the chickpeas and place them in a large pan or pressure cooker. Cover with water and bring to the boil. Reduce the heat and simmer over a medium heat for about 30 minutes to 1 hour, until tender. Reserve 60 ml / 2 fl oz (^{1}/$_4$ cup) cooking liquid, then drain. Keep warm.

2 Mix the crushed garlic with the salt and dried mint. Fry in butter for about 3 to 5 minutes until lightly browned. Remove from the heat and transfer to a bowl. Strain the yoghurt and mix it into the fried garlic.

3 Place the toasted bread in a large serving dish. Add the cooked chickpeas with the reserved cooking liquid and top with the yoghurt. Sprinkle with dried mint, paprika and pine nuts. Serve immediately.

JORDAN

SERVES 4

3 Tbsp olive oil
3 green peppers, cut into long strips
1 small chilli pepper, diced (optional)
3 garlic cloves, peeled and crushed
3 medium tomatoes, chopped
Salt and black pepper, to taste
1 Tbsp ground coriander (optional)

Shakshoukeh
Green peppers with tomatoes

1 Heat the olive oil in a pan and add the green peppers, chilli pepper and garlic. Fry for 3 minutes until tender. Stir in the tomatoes, salt, pepper and ground coriander, if using. Cover and simmer over a low heat for 5 to 7 minutes until most of the juice has evaporated. Serve cold.

Chickpeas in yoghurt sauce

EGYPT

MAKES 45 PATTIES

For the patties
225 g / 8 oz (1 cup) dry shelled broad
  beans, soaked overnight
225 g / 8 oz (1 cup) dry chickpeas, soaked
  overnight
4 Tbsp parsley, roughly chopped
4 Tbsp mint, roughly chopped
4 Tbsp fresh coriander, roughly chopped
1 medium onion, peeled and chopped
2 garlic cloves, peeled and crushed
1 tsp dried coriander
1 tsp cumin
1/2 tsp turmeric
1/2 tsp cayenne
2 tsp salt
1 tsp bicarbonate of soda
Vegetable oil for deep-frying

For the dip
125 ml / 4 fl oz (1/2 cup) tahini
125 ml / 4 fl oz (1/2 cup) lemon juice
240 ml / 8 fl oz (1 cup) water
1 tsp salt

Pickles and pitta bread, to serve
Parsley sprigs and mint, to garnish

Falafel
Fried chickpea patties

1 Start by making the patties. Drain the broad beans and chickpeas and place in a food processor with the parsley, mint, fresh coriander, onion, garlic, all the spices and salt. Process to a firm paste. Transfer to a mixing bowl and add the bicarbonate of soda. Knead to combine thoroughly and leave to rest for 1 hour.

2 Heat the vegetable oil in a heavy-based frying pan. When the paste has rested, knead it again with your hands and shape it into walnut-size balls, then flatten slightly. Gently lower the patties into the hot oil, a few at a time, and deep fry for about 5 to 6 minutes.

3 Remove the patties from the oil and drain them on paper towels. Repeat with remaining patties.

4 To make the tahini dip, mix all the dip ingredients together in a small bowl. Serve the falafel either hot or cold with the tahini dip, along with some pickles and pitta bread. Garnish with snipped parsley and mint.

LEBANON

SERVES 3–4

500 g / 1 lb 2 oz vine leaves
1 medium potato, peeled and cut into thick slices
1 medium onion, peeled and cut into thick rings
1 medium tomato, cut into thick slices

For the stuffing
360 g / 12$^{1}/_{2}$ oz (4 cups) parsley
1 medium onion, peeled and chopped
Salt, to taste
$^{1}/_{2}$ tsp white pepper
150 g / 5$^{1}/_{2}$ oz ($^{3}/_{4}$ cup) short grain rice, rinsed and drained
3 medium tomatoes, rinsed and chopped
60 ml / 2 fl oz ($^{1}/_{4}$ cup) lemon juice
85 ml / 3 fl oz ($^{1}/_{3}$ cup) olive oil

Warak inab bil zeit
Stuffed vine leaves

1 Remove and discard the vine leave stems. Place the vine leaves in boiling water, remove immediately, then drain.

2 To prepare the stuffing, remove and discard the thick stalks of parsley. Chop the parsley as finely as possible and place it in a large bowl. Rub the onion with the salt and pepper and add to the bowl. Add in the rice, tomatoes, lemon juice and olive oil and toss.

3 Line a deep pan with the potato slices, onion rings and half the tomato slices. Place a generous tablespoon of stuffing in the centre of each vine leaf, on the stem side. Fold the sides of the leaf over the stuffing, then roll up firmly but not too tightly. Repeat with remaining leaves.

4 Pack the rolls flap-side down in the pan. Top with the remaining tomato slices. Add water to cover the rolls, then place a plate on top of the rolls to keep them intact during cooking. Bring to the boil, then reduce the heat and simmer gently for 45 minutes, until the rice is tender. Serve cold.

 LEBANON

SERVES 3–4

1 kg / 2 lb 3 oz green broad beans
125 ml / 4 fl oz ($^{1}/_{2}$ cup) olive oil
2 large onions, peeled and chopped
Salt, to taste
250 ml / 8$^{1}/_{3}$ fl oz (1 cup) water
4 garlic cloves, peeled and crushed
90 g / 3 oz (1 cup) fresh coriander, chopped
Juice of 1 lemon

Foul bi zeit
Green broad beans in olive oil

1 Rinse the broad beans. Cut off the ends and remove the strings. Cut into medium-size pieces.

2 Reserve 1 tablespoon olive oil for later use and heat the remaining quantity in a saucepan, then add the onions. Cook over a low heat, stirring frequently until tender, for about 10 minutes.

3 Add the broad beans to the onions and cook for about 10 minutes, stirring frequently. Season with salt to taste. Add the water to the pan, then cover and simmer for 20 minutes until the beans are tender.

Stuffed vine leaves

4 In a separate frying pan, fry the garlic and coriander in reserved olive oil for 2 to 3 minutes until the garlic is golden brown. Add to the broad bean saucepan. Stir in the lemon juice and simmer for an additional 5 minutes. Serve hot or cold.

LEBANON

SERVES 4–6

3 Tbsp olive oil
2 medium onions, peeled and chopped
2 garlic cloves, peeled and crushed
1 kg / 2 lb 3 oz fresh green beans, cut into
    medium-size pieces
1/2 tsp salt
1/4 tsp cinnamon
1/2 tsp black pepper
4 medium tomatoes, chopped
250 ml / 9 fl oz (1 cup) water
2 Tbsp fresh lemon juice
Green salad and pitta bread, to serve

Loubieh bil banadoora

Green beans in tomato sauce

1 Heat the olive oil in a large frying pan. Add the onions and garlic and cook until tender. Add the green beans and leave to simmer gently for 15 minutes, stirring occasionally. Season with salt, cinnamon and pepper.

2 Stir in the tomatoes, water and lemon juice and bring to the boil. Reduce the heat, cover and simmer for 30 minutes until tender. Adjust the seasoning if necessary. Serve hot or cold with a green salad and pitta bread.

 SYRIA

SERVES 6

3 Tbsp olive oil
1 large onion, peeled and thinly sliced
2 garlic cloves, peeled and crushed
420 g / 15 oz (1 1/2 cups) canned cooked
    chickpeas
60 g / 2 oz (1/2 cup) walnuts, coarsely
    chopped
500 g / 1 lb 2 oz cabbage, finely chopped
Salt, to taste
1/4 tsp cinnamon
1/4 tsp cumin
125 ml / 4 fl oz (1/2 cup) lemon juice

Makmoura

Cabbage with chickpeas

1 Heat the olive oil in a frying pan, then add the onion. Fry over a moderate heat for 5 minutes until tender. Add the garlic, stirring for 3 minutes, then add the chickpeas and walnuts, and cook for a further 5 minutes.

2 Stir in the cabbage. Cover and cook for 10 to 12 minutes until the cabbage is tender. Season with salt, cinnamon and cumin. Finally, stir in the lemon juice. Serve hot or cold.

SYRIA

SERVES 4–5

150 g / 5¹/2 oz (1 cup) fine burghul
  (fine cracked wheat)
45 g /1¹/2 oz (¹/4 cup) plain flour
1 tsp salt
4 spring onions with tops, chopped
4 Tbsp mint, chopped
4 Tbsp parsley, chopped
400 g / 14 oz (2 cups) lentils
4 garlic cloves, peeled and crushed
3 Tbsp olive oil
3 Tbsp pomegranate molasses,
  or juice of 3 lemons

Kibbeh hili
Vegetarian kibbeh

1 Mix the burghul, flour, ¹/2 teaspoon salt, green onions, mint and parsley in a bowl. Add enough water and knead with wet hands to a firm dough. Roll the dough into firmly-packed balls the size of large cherries and set aside.

2 Place the lentils in a pot, add 2 litres / 70 fl oz (8 cups) water and bring to the boil for 20 minutes. Add the remaining salt, reduce the heat and simmer for about 15 minutes until tender.

3 Add the dough balls, garlic and olive oil to the pot. Simmer for a further 15 minutes until the balls are tender. Stir in the pomegranate molasses or lemon juice. Serve hot.

 BAHRAIN

SERVES 4

4 Tbsp olive oil
2 medium onions, peeled and sliced
3 garlic cloves, peeled and crushed
1 large carrot, peeled and cut into thick slices
2 large courgettes, cut into thick slices
1 aubergine, cubed
2 turnips, cubed
¹/2 small cauliflower, divided into florets
1 medium potato, cubed
100 g / 3¹/2 oz pumpkin, cubed
100 g / 3¹/2 oz green beans, cut into
  small pieces
200 g / 7 oz spinach, chopped
1 tsp paprika
1 tsp turmeric
1 tsp dried lime or lemon peel
Salt and black pepper, to taste
420 g / 15 oz (1¹/2 cups) canned cooked
  chickpeas (optional)
2 medium tomatoes, quartered
250 ml / 9 fl oz (1 cup) hot water or
  chicken stock

Salona al khidar
Vegetable stew

1 Heat the olive oil in a heavy-based saucepan. Add the onions and garlic and fry for 2 minutes. Add all the other vegetables (minus the chickpeas and tomatoes) and spices. Mix together, cover and simmer over a low heat for 40 minutes until all vegetables are tender. Stir frequently.

2 Add the chickpeas, chopped tomatoes and water or chicken stock. Bring to the boil, then reduce the heat. Simmer for 10 to 15 minutes. Serve hot with boiled rice.

SAUDI ARABIA

MAKES 45 PIECES

For the kibbeh paste
1 kg / 2 lb 3 oz potatoes
750 g /1 lb 10 oz (5 cups) fine burghul
(fine cracked wheat)
Pinch of salt
1/2 tsp marjoram
1/2 tsp black pepper
125 g / 4 oz (3/4 cup) plain flour
250 ml / 81/3 fl oz (1 cup) vegetable oil,
for frying

For the filling
150 g / 51/2 oz black and green olives,
pitted and chopped
60 g / 2 oz (1/2 cup) walnuts, coarsely
chopped
4 garlic cloves, peeled and crushed
2 Tbsp olive oil
1 tsp sumac
1/2 tsp marjoram
1/4 tsp ground hot pepper

Kibbeh al batatos
Potato cakes

1 Start by making the kibbeh paste. Boil the potatoes until tender, then peel and mash them to a purée and set aside.

2 Thoroughly rinse the burghul. Place in a bowl, cover with water and leave to soak for 5 minutes. Drain, then squeeze to remove as much water as possible. Combine the burghul with the puréed potatoes, salt, marjoram, pepper and flour until well blended and set aside.

3 To make the filling, rinse the black and green olives to remove some of the salt. Place them in a small bowl. Add the walnuts, garlic, olive oil, sumac and marjoram.

4 Shape the potato and burghul mixture into balls the size of small eggs. Hollow out the centre of each ball using your finger. Work your finger around the hole until you have a thin oval shell. Fill the shell with 1 tablespoon of filling, then pinch the opening with damp fingers to close and shape into ovals. Place in a large tray. Repeat until all the quantity is finished.

5 Heat the oil in a pan. Deep fry the balls in small batches until browned on all sides, for about 7 to 10 minutes. Remove them from the oil and drain. Serve warm.

BAHRAIN

SERVES 5–6

1/2 tsp saffron threads
3 Tbsp rose water
150 g / 51/2 oz (3/4 cup) caster sugar
2.5 litres / 5.3 pints (101/2 cups) water
500 g / 1 lb 2 oz (21/2 cups) basmati or
  long grain rice
3 Tbsp butter
1/4 tsp ground cardamom
Fried fish, to serve

Muhammar
Golden rice

1 Soak the saffron in the rose water and set aside.

2 Place the sugar in a pan and heat over a medium heat until melted and golden brown. Add the water and bring to the boil. Stir in the rice and bring to the boil again. Cook uncovered for 10 minutes until the rice is half cooked, then drain.

3 In a separate pan, heat the butter, then add the cooked rice. Pour in the saffron-rose water and add the cardamom. Cover and simmer very gently for 25 to 30 minutes until tender. Serve with fried fish.

 LEBANON

SERVES 4–6

400 g / 14 oz (2 cups) lentils
1250 ml / 2.6 pints (5 cups) water
125 ml / 4 fl oz (1/2 cup) olive oil
2 large onions, peeled and thinly sliced
200 g / 7 oz (11/3 cups) coarse burghul
  (coarse cracked wheat)
Salt, to taste
Pickles and salad, to serve

Mjadra
Lentils with cracked wheat

1 Rinse the lentils and place them in a saucepan with the water and bring to the boil. Reduce the heat, cover and simmer over a low heat for 30 minutes.

2 In the meantime, heat the olive oil in a frying pan and fry the onions over a moderate heat for about 10 minutes, until dark brown. Add 235 ml / 8 fl oz (1 cup) of water to the pan. Simmer over a moderate heat for about 10 minutes, until tender, then remove from the heat. Crush the onions with a fork and add them with the oil from the pan to the saucepan of lentils.

3 Thoroughly rinse the burghul and add it to the lentils. Cover and simmer gently for about 15 minutes until most of the water is absorbed and the lentils and burghul are tender. Add more hot water if necessary.

4 Transfer to a serving dish. Serve hot or cold with pickles and salad.

Golden rice

JORDAN

SERVES 5

200 g / 7 oz (1 cup) dry chickpeas
1/2 tsp bicarbonate of soda
3 large aubergines
125 ml / 4 fl oz (1/2 cup) olive oil
750 g / 1 lb 10 oz tomatoes
250 ml / 9 fl oz (1 cup) vegetable oil
12 small onions, peeled and left whole
5 garlic cloves, peeled and crushed
2 Tbsp tomato paste
470 ml / 16 fl oz (2 cups) water
Salt and white pepper, to taste

Moussaka'a bi zeit

Cooked aubergines

1 Rinse the chickpeas, cover with water, add the bicarbonate of soda and soak overnight. The next day, thoroughly rinse the chickpeas. Place them in a saucepan or pressure cooker, cover with water and bring to the boil. Then turn down the heat and simmer until tender, for between 30 minutes to 1 hour.

2 Peel the aubergines, slice them lengthways and season them with salt. Heat the olive oil in a frying pan and fry the aubergine slices until brown on both sides. Drain on absorbent paper.

3 Cut half the tomatoes into cubes and the other half into slices. Heat the olive oil in a frying pan and fry the onions and garlic until tender. Add the cubed tomatoes and chickpeas and cook for 5 minutes over a medium heat.

4 Preheat the oven to 180° C / 350° F. Place the aubergine slices in a 28 x 33-cm (11 x 13-in) oven-proof dish, add the onion and chickpea mixture and top with tomato slices.

5 Dissolve the tomato paste in the water and pour evenly over the baking dish. Sprinkle with salt and pepper. Bake for 35 minutes. Serve cold.

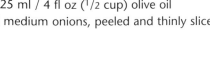 **LEBANON**

SERVES 4–6

400 g / 14 oz (2 cups) lentils
1250 ml / 2.6 pints (5 cups) water
200 g / 7 oz (1 cup) short grain rice
Salt, to taste
125 ml / 4 fl oz ($^1/_2$ cup) olive oil
4 medium onions, peeled and thinly sliced

Mdardara
Lentils with rice

1 Rinse the lentils and place them in a pan with the water. Bring to the boil, then reduce the heat. Cover and simmer for 30 minutes until the lentils are almost tender.

2 Rinse the rice and add it to the lentils with the salt. Simmer over a low heat for about 15 minutes.

3 In the meantime, heat the olive oil in a frying pan and fry the onions over a moderate heat until golden brown. Set aside one third of the quantity for garnishing.

4 Add the remaining onion and oil to the pan of lentils. Simmer for 10 minutes until all the liquid is absorbed and the rice and lentils are tender.

5 Transfer to a serving dish and garnish with the reserved browned onions. Serve hot or cold with salad.

 EGYPT

SERVES 4–6

1 kg / 2 lb 3 oz canned cooked broad beans
3 garlic cloves, peeled
$^1/_2$ tsp salt
Juice of 2 lemons
3 Tbsp olive oil
Pinch of cumin
2 Tbsp chopped parsley and
  1 medium chopped tomato, to garnish
Bread, to serve

Foul medammas
Simmered broad beans

1 Place the broad beans with their liquid in a pot and bring to the boil. Reduce the heat and simmer for 5 minutes, then remove from heat.

2 In a bowl, crush the garlic with the salt. Mix in the lemon juice, olive oil and cumin. Add this mixture to the beans.

3 Transfer the beans to a serving dish. Garnish with chopped parsley and tomato. Serve warm or cold with bread.

Lentils with rice

MEAT

Popular Middle-Eastern meats include beef, lamb and goat. Pork is rarely used as it is disallowed by religion. The following pages are filled with sensational recipes that are perfect for any occasion. Tender and flavoursome lamb is king of the table. It can be braised, roasted whole, layered with dough, cooked with yoghurt or milk, or combined with vegetables and grains. Cut it into chunks or strips, or mince it with parsley and spices to make delicious Kofta (page 70) or Spiced grilled steaks (page 72). Kibbeh, or Minced meat with cracked wheat (page 54), the national dish of the Lebanon, is definitely one to try. Whatever your choice, always use the best cuts and never compromise on quality.

LEBANON

SERVES 4

For the stuffing
2 medium onions, peeled and finely chopped
2 Tbsp vegetable oil
60 g / 2 oz ($^1/_3$ cup) pine nuts
250 g / 9 oz beef or lamb, coarsely minced
$^1/_2$ tsp of each: salt, black pepper, allspice
  and cinnamon
1 tsp sumac (optional)

For the meat mixture
500 g / 1 lb 2 oz extra lean beef or lamb,
  from the leg
1 medium onion, peeled and finely chopped
1 tsp salt
$^1/_2$ tsp of each: allspice, black pepper and
  cinnamon
1 tsp marjoram (optional)
300 g / 10$^1/_2$ oz (2 cups) fine burghul
  (fine cracked wheat), washed and drained
4 crushed ice cubes
3 Tbsp butter, for greasing
125 ml / 4 fl oz ($^1/_2$ cup) olive or corn oil
Green salad, to serve

Kibbeh bel saynieh
Baked minced meat with cracked wheat

1 Start by making the stuffing. Fry the onions in the vegetable oil until tender. Add the pine nuts and fry gently until golden brown. Add the meat and cook until all the juices have evaporated and the meat begins to brown. Season with salt and all the spices. Remove the stuffing from the heat and set aside until needed.

2 To make the meat mixture, trim all the fat and fine skin from the meat, then cut into small pieces. Place half the meat in a food processor and process until paste-like in consistency. Transfer to a large bowl, process the remaining meat in the same manner, then transfer this second batch to the bowl.

3 Process the onion with the salt and add to the meat. Then add in all the spices, the marjoram, if using, and the burghul, and knead to a smooth paste with wet hands.

4 Transfer the meat mixture to the food processor and process again in four batches, adding a tablespoon of crushed ice each time, until the meat paste reaches a very smooth consistency. Combine again in a bowl and knead well with moistened hands for about 1 minute.

5 Preheat the oven to 200° C / 400° F. Divide the meat mixture into 2 portions. Brush a 30-cm (12-in) round baking dish with the butter. Spread half the mixture onto the base, smoothing it with wet hands. Top with the stuffing made earlier, spreading it evenly over the base. Divide remaining half into five pieces. Flatten each piece with wet hands and cover the stuffing with these pieces. Carefully press them out with wet hands to make an even surface.

6 Make deep criss-cross lines on the surface with a sharp knife, then run the knife blade around the sides of the baking dish to avoid the kibbeh sticking to the sides. Make a hole in the centre with your forefinger and pour the oil over the top. Bake for 30 minutes. Serve hot with a green salad.

LEBANON

SERVES 6

1.5 kg / 3 lb 5 oz leg of lamb
1 garlic clove, peeled
Salt, to taste
2 Tbsp corn oil
2 Tbsp white wine vinegar
1 Tbsp oregano
1/2 tsp allspice
1/2 tsp cinnamon
1/2 tsp black pepper
125 g / 4 oz (1/2 cup) butter
2 carrots, peeled
5 small onions, peeled
2 Tbsp plain flour
400 g / 14 oz (2 cups) long grain rice
1 large onion, peeled and finely chopped
500 g / 1 lb 2 oz minced lamb
2 beef stock cubes
60 g / 2 oz (1/3 cup) pine nuts
60 g / 2 oz (1/3 cup) blanched almonds
60 g / 2 oz (1/3 cup) pistachio nuts
Roasted tomatoes, to garnish

Fakhda bil forn

Roast leg of lamb

1 Trim any excess fat from the leg of lamb. In a bowl, pound the garlic with 1 teaspoon salt and brush the lamb with this paste.

2 In a separate bowl, combine the corn oil, vinegar, oregano, 1/4 teaspoon allspice, cinnamon and black pepper, and brush the lamb with this mixture. Refrigerate for 2 hours or overnight.

3 Preheat the oven to 190° C / 375° F. Heat the butter in a large frying pan. Fry the lamb for 5 minutes on each side, then transfer to a baking dish. Cook in the oven for about 1 1/2 to 2 hours until tender and brown. Baste occasionally with the juices in the dish. After 1 hour of cooking, add the whole carrots and small onions. Remove from the oven and keep the leg of lamb in a warm place, reserving the juices.

4 To make the sauce, stir the flour into the juices in the baking dish. Add 475 ml / 16 fl oz (2 cups) water and bring to the boil. Simmer over a low heat for 3 minutes. Strain and keep aside.

5 Thoroughly rinse the rice and soak in warm water for 30 minutes. In a frying pan, fry the chopped onion in 1 tablespoon butter until golden brown, then stir in the minced lamb and leave over a moderate heat until brown. Season with salt and the remaining allspice, cinnamon and black pepper. Add 950 ml / 32 fl oz (4 cups) water, the beef stock cubes and rice to the pan. Cover and simmer gently until tender.

6 Brown the nuts in 2 tablespoons corn oil. To serve, pour the rice in a serving platter and arrange sliced lamb pieces on top. Garnish with roasted tomatoes and sprinkle with the nuts. Serve with the sauce.

LEBANON

SERVES 4

For the stuffing

2 medium onions, peeled and chopped
4 tsp vegetable oil
45 g / 1 1/2 oz (1/4 cup) pine nuts
250 g / 9 oz beef or lamb, coarsely minced
1/2 tsp of each: salt, black pepper, allspice
  and ground cinnamon
1 tsp sumac (optional)

For the meat shells

500 g / 1 lb 2 oz extra lean beef or lamb,
  from the leg
1 medium onion, peeled and finely chopped
1 tsp salt
1/2 tsp each of: allspice, black pepper and
  cinnamon
300 g / 10 1/2 oz (2 cups) fine burghul
  (fine cracked wheat), rinsed and drained
4 crushed ice cubes
1 tsp marjoram (optional)
250 ml / 9 fl oz (1 cup) vegetable oil,
  for frying
Salad, to serve

Kibbeh kbaibat

Fried kibbeh

1 Start by making the stuffing. Fry the onions in the vegetable oil until tender. Add the pine nuts and fry gently until golden brown. Add the meat and cook until all the juices have evaporated and the meat begins to brown. Season with the salt, black pepper, spices and sumac, if using. Remove the stuffing from the heat and set aside.

2 To prepare the meat shells, trim all the fat and fine skin from the meat and cut into cubes. Using a food processor, process half the meat to a paste-like consistency, then transfer to a large bowl. Process the remaining meat in the same manner.

3 Process the onion with the salt and add to the meat. Add the spices and burghul to the mixture and knead to a homogeneous paste with moistened hands. Process again in four batches, adding a tablespoon of crushed ice each time and the marjoram, if using. The kibbeh paste should be very smooth. Combine again in a bowl and knead well with moistened hands for about 1 minute.

4 Divide the meat mixture into 20 to 25 egg-size portions and roll into balls. Make a hole in the ball using your forefinger. Work your finger around the hole, pressing gently until you have a thin oval shell. Fill the shell with the stuffing, pinch to close and place on a tray.

5 Heat the vegetable oil in a pan until hot. Deep-fry the kibbeh shells in batches until browned on all sides. Lift out with a slotted spoon and drain on paper towels. Serve hot with a salad. It can also be served cold as a starter.

JORDAN

SERVES 4–5

3 garlic cloves, peeled crushed
1 tsp salt
60 ml / 2 fl oz (^{1}/4 cup) lemon juice
60 ml / 2 fl oz (^{1}/4 cup) olive oil
1 kg /2 lb 3 oz lamb from the leg, cubed
^{1}/2 tsp black pepper
1 tsp dried oregano
2 large green peppers, cubed
4 medium tomatoes, cut into wedges
4 large onions, peeled and cut into wedges
Salad and bread, to serve

Shish kebab
Lamb kebabs

1 In a small bowl, pound the garlic with the salt until it forms a soft paste. Stir in the lemon juice and the olive oil. Add the meat cubes, black pepper and oregano. Toss to coat and marinate in the refrigerator for 2 hours or overnight.

2 Thread the meat onto skewers, alternating with green pepper, tomato and onion wedges. Grill the kebabs over glowing charcoal for 8 to 10 minutes, turning frequently and brushing with marinade so that all sides are coated. Serve hot with salad and bread.

 LEBANON

SERVES 5

3 large aubergines
375 ml / 12.5 fl oz (1 cup) vegetable oil
75 g / 2^1/2 oz (^{1}/2 cup) pine nuts
500 g / 1 lb 2 oz minced lamb or beef
Salt and black pepper, to taste
400 g / 14 oz (2 cups) long grain rice
2 medium tomatoes, sliced
2 Tbsp tomato paste
1 litre / 35 fl oz (4^1/3 cups) hot water

Makloubit batinjan
Upside-down aubergine

1 Cut the aubergines lengthways into 1-cm (^{1}/2-in) thick slices. Deep fry in the vegetable oil until golden brown, then drain on absorbent paper.

2 In a separate pan, fry the pine nuts in 2 tablespoons vegetable oil until golden brown. Add the minced meat and cook until browned, then season to taste.

3 Preheat the oven to 190° C / 375° F. Rinse the rice several times until the water runs clear, then drain. Place half the quantity of tomato slices in the base of a deep 30-cm (12-in) round oven-proof pan. Arrange half the aubergine slices over the tomatoes. Top with half the meat and half the rice. Repeat with the remaining ingredients.

4 Dissolve the tomato paste in the hot water and add it to the pan. Season to taste. Cover and cook in the oven for 30 minutes, then remove the pan from the oven and cool for 5 minutes. Carefully invert onto a large serving dish. Sprinkle with the pine nuts and serve hot.

Upside-down aubergine

UNITED ARAB EMIRATES

SERVES 20

1 small whole lamb, weighing about 10 kg /
  22 lb, trimmed and rinsed
1 lemon, halved
Salt, to taste
60 g / 2 oz (¹/4 cup) baharat spices
  (see page 158)
2 tsp turmeric
2 tsp saffron threads, pounded and soaked
  in 125 ml / 4 fl oz (¹/2 cup) rose water
1 kg / 2 lb 3 oz (5 cups) long grain rice
200 g / 7 oz (1 cup) ghee or shortening
3 large onions, peeled and finely chopped
1 kg / 2 lb 3 oz minced lamb
1250 ml / 2.6 pints (5 cups) water
200 g / 7 oz (1 cup) blanched almonds
200 g / 7 oz (1 cup) pine nuts
100 g / 3¹/2 oz (¹/2 cup) pistachio nuts
100 g / 3¹/2 oz (¹/2 cup) raisins

Kouzi

Whole lamb

1 Rub the whole lamb with the lemon halves. Season with salt, half the baharat, and 1 teaspoon turmeric. Put aside. Soak the saffron threads in the rose water for 30 minutes. Rinse the rice under cold running water and drain.

2 In a large pan, melt half the ghee or shortening and add the onions. Fry gently until tender, then add the minced lamb and cook until browned. Add in remaining baharat, turmeric and rice. Stir for 5 minutes over a medium heat, then add the water and bring to the boil, stirring occasionally. Add salt to taste, reduce the heat, then cover and simmer over a low heat for 10 minutes.

3 Fry the nuts in 3 tablespoons ghee until golden brown. Add the nuts and raisins to the rice. Sprinkle half the rose water mixture over the rice mixture. Cover the pan and leave off the heat for 20 minutes until the liquid has been absorbed.

4 Preheat the oven to 190° C / 375° F. Fill the lamb cavity with the rice mixture, then sew up the cavity with string and a thick needle. Truss the lamb by tying the hind shank to the foreshank. Place a large rack in a very large baking dish and arrange the lamb on the rack. Brush the lamb with the remaining ghee. Cover the dish with aluminium foil, pressing the foil under the edges to seal completely.

5 Bake for 4 to 5 hours, basting occasionally with the juices and the remaining rose water. When the meat becomes very tender, remove the foil and brown the lamb. Transfer the lamb on to a very large platter, remove the string and spoon the stuffing out on a platter. Serve hot.

JORDAN

SERVES 6

1 kg / 2 lb 3 oz lamb chunks from
  the shoulder
Salt and black pepper, to taste
60 ml / 2 fl oz (1/4 cup) vegetable oil
45 g / 1 1/2 oz (1/4 cup) pine nuts
90 g / 3 oz (1/2 cup) blanched almonds
2 medium onions, peeled and chopped
1 1/2 tsp turmeric
1/2 tsp ground allspice
1 tsp cinnamon
1 litre / 35 fl oz (4 1/3 cups) yoghurt
1 medium egg
1 Tbsp cornflour
4 slices flat bread or pitta bread

Mansaf

Seasoned lamb in yoghurt

1 Place the lamb chunks in a large saucepan and cover with cold water. Slowly bring to the boil, skimming as required. Add salt and black pepper to taste, cover and simmer gently for 30 minutes.

2 Heat 1 tablespoon vegetable oil in a frying pan and add the pine nuts and almonds. Fry until golden brown, then remove and drain. Discard the oil.

3 Heat another 2 tablespoons vegetable oil in the same frying pan, add the onions and cook gently until tender. Stir in the turmeric, allspice and cinnamon and cook for 1 minute. Add this mixture to the lamb.

4 Place the yoghurt in a bowl. Beat the egg with a fork and blend it into the yoghurt. Dissolve the cornflour in 3 tablespoons cold water. Add to the yoghurt mixture with 1 teaspoon salt, stirring well. Pass through a sieve into a heavy-based saucepan.

5 Place the yoghurt mixture over a medium heat, stirring constantly with a wooden spoon in the same direction. When it begins to boil, reduce the heat and leave to simmer gently uncovered for 5 minutes until thick, stirring occasionally.

6 After 1 hour of cooking, uncover the lamb saucepan and allow the liquid to evaporate until it half covers the lamb. Add the yoghurt mixture, stirring well. Simmer gently until the lamb is tender and the sauce thickens.

7 To serve in the traditional manner, place the bread on a serving platter, cover with cooked rice, then pour the yoghurt sauce and meat pieces over the bread. Garnish with the pine nuts and almonds.

JORDAN

SERVES 4–6

1 large cabbage
9 garlic cloves, unpeeled
950 ml / 32 fl oz (4 cups) water
1 beef stock cube
Juice of 1 lemon
Salt, to taste
1 Tbsp butter or vegetable oil
3 garlic cloves, peeled crushed
1 tsp dried mint

For the stuffing
500 g / 1 lb 2 oz minced beef or lamb
300 g / 10^1/$_2$ oz (1^1/$_2$ cups) short grain rice
3 Tbsp vegetable oil or butter
1 tsp salt
^{1}/$_4$ tsp of each: allspice, cinnamon and
  black pepper

Yoghurt, to serve

Malfouf mahshi
Stuffed cabbage rolls

1 Start by preparing the cabbage. Carefully remove the cabbage leaves, then rinse and place them in a large pan. Cover the leaves with hot water and bring to the boil for 3 minutes until soft and pliable, then drain. Cut the leaves into halves lengthways to remove the hard stalks. Keep the stalks for later use.

2 To make the stuffing, mix all stuffing ingredients together. Place a quantity of filling the size of a forefinger on the narrow edge of a cabbage leaf. Fold over the sides and roll neatly. Repeat until all the ingredients are used up. Place the cabbage rolls, seam-side down, in layers in a deep pan lined with unused cabbage leaves and stalks. Arrange the unpeeled garlic cloves amongst the cabbage roll layers.

3 Pour the water over the rolls, add the beef stock cube, lemon juice and salt to taste. Cover with an inverted dish to prevent the rolls floating and bring to the boil. Reduce the heat and simmer until tender, for about 45 to 50 minutes.

4 Heat butter or vegetable oil in a pan. Add the crushed garlic and mint. Fry until golden brown. Pour the garlic mixture over the cabbage rolls and cook for a further 10 minutes. Place the cabbage rolls neatly in a serving dish. Serve hot with yoghurt.

 LEBANON

SERVES 5

For the meat
1 kg / 2 lb 3 oz shoulder of lamb
^{1}/$_4$ tsp of each: allspice, cinnamon and
  black pepper
750 ml / 1^1/$_2$ pints (3 cups) water

Dali'i mahshi
Stuffed lamb shoulder

1 Start by preparing the meat. Cut an opening on one side of the shoulder for stuffing. Rinse the shoulder and pat dry. Rub with all the spices.

2 To make the stuffing, brown the pine nuts in a frying pan in 1 tablespoon butter. Lift and drain. Brown the minced meat in 1 tablespoon butter. Season with the salt and all the spices. Rinse the rice and add to the minced meat.

For the stuffing

60 g / 2 oz (¹/3 cup) pine nuts
45 g / 1¹/2 oz butter
250 g / 9 oz minced beef or lamb
1 tsp salt
¹/2 tsp of each: allspice, cinnamon and
  black pepper
200 g / 7 oz (1 cup) long grain rice
1 carrot, peeled
1 celery stick
1 cinnamon stick
1 bay leaf
Salt, to taste

Cook over a medium heat for 3 minutes, stirring constantly, then add the browned pine nuts.

3 Fill the opening in the shoulder with this stuffing. Close with the help of string and a thick needle or with bamboo skewers. Place in a pan. Add water to the shoulder and bring to the boil, skimming as necessary. Add the carrot, celery, cinnamon stick, bay leaf and salt. Reduce the heat and cook for 2 hours until the meat is tender.

4 Preheat the oven to 200° C / 400° F. Lift the meat from the pan and place it in an oven dish. Brush with butter and brown in the oven on both sides for 1 hour. Place the shoulder on a large platter. Remove the string and cut into large chunks. Serve hot with the stuffing.

IRAQ

SERVES 8–10

For the vegetables
5 red peppers
5 green peppers
15 small aubergines
15 small courgettes
6 small potatoes
500 g / 1 lb 2 oz vine leaves
500 ml / 17 fl oz (2 cups) hot water
750 ml / 1 1/2 pints (3 cups) chicken stock
2 Tbsp lemon juice

For the stuffing
1.5 kg / 3 lb 5 oz minced beef or lamb
800 g / 1 lb 12 oz short grain rice
90 g / 3 oz (1 cup) parsley, chopped
90 g / 3 oz (1 cup) fresh coriander, chopped
2 medium tomatoes, diced
2 medium onions, finely chopped
3 garlic cloves, peeled and crushed
100 g / 3 1/2 oz butter
1/2 tsp of each: black pepper, cumin
  and allspice
1 Tbsp salt

Dolmas
Stuffed vegetables

1 Start by preparing the vegetables. Thoroughly rinse all the vegetables. Cut the tops off the peppers and remove the seeds and white membrane, then rinse and drain. Cut the tops off the potatoes. Cut the stems and tops off the aubergines and courgettes. Scoop out the flesh of the potatoes, aubergines and courgettes using a special scooping tool or a spoon, leaving 5 mm (1/4 in) of the flesh. Be careful not to break the shells while scooping. Rinse and drain. Soak the vine leaves in the hot water for 10 minutes. Drain and remove the stems.

2 To make the stuffing, thoroughly combine all the ingredients in a large bowl. Fill the peppers, aubergines, courgettes and potato shells with the stuffing. Do not fill the vegetables completely as there should be enough space for the rice to expand.

3 Place an amount of stuffing the size of a small finger in the middle of a vine leaf on the stem side. Fold the sides of the vine leaf over the stuffing, then roll it up firmly but not too tightly. Repeat until all the stuffing is finished. Neatly arrange the stuffed vine leaves in a large dish.

4 Place any unused vine leaves in the bottom of a large heavy-based saucepan. Arrange the stuffed potatoes and peppers in an upright position in the pan. Place the aubergines and courgettes horizontally on top of the potatoes and peppers and arrange the stuffed vine leaves on top.

5 Pour 125 ml / 4 fl oz (1/2 cup) of the chicken stock, the lemon juice and water to cover, over the stuffed vegetables. Cover with a plate to keep them in place. Bring to the boil, then reduce the heat. Simmer gently until most of the liquid has been absorbed. Gradually add the remaining chicken stock and simmer gently for 1 1/2 hours. Carefully remove the dolmas from the pan and arrange them in a serving dish. Serve hot.

KUWAIT

SERVES 8

200 g / 7 oz (1 cup) shelled wheat
2 kg / 4 lb 6 oz lamb shoulder on the bone,
  cut into large chunks
10 cardamom pods
1 cinnamon stick
3 cloves
1 small onion, peeled
1 parsley sprig
1 tsp salt
800 g / 1 lb 12 oz (4 cups) basmati or
  long grain rice
2 Tbsp butter
5 medium onions, peeled and finely chopped
1/2 tsp turmeric
1/4 tsp ground cardamom
1/4 tsp black pepper
2 medium tomatoes, chopped
1 tsp saffron threads, soaked in 235 ml /
  8 fl oz (1 cup) of water

Machbous

Spiced lamb and rice

1 Place the wheat in a heavy-based saucepan or pressure cooker with 2 litres / 70 fl oz (8 cups) of cold water. Bring to the boil, then cover and simmer over a medium heat for 45 minutes to 1 1/2 hours until tender.

2 In the meantime, rinse the meat several times. Place in a large saucepan and cover with water. Bring to the boil, skimming as necessary. Add the cardamom pods, cinnamon stick, clove, whole onion and parsley sprig. Cover and simmer for 45 minutes. Season with the salt when meat is cooked.

3 Rinse the rice several times until the water runs clear and soak in water for 30 minutes.

4 In a large saucepan, gently fry the onions in butter until tender. Stir in the turmeric and cook for 2 minutes. Add 125 ml / 4 fl oz (1/2 cup) of water and bring to the boil. Stir in the ground cardamom, black pepper, tomatoes, wheat and rice and simmer for 10 minutes. Cover the rice and wheat mixture with 700 ml / 24 fl oz (3 cups) of the meat stock. Simmer for 20 minutes, stirring twice during cooking. When cooked, sprinkle with the saffron water. Add the meat and simmer gently for 20 minutes. Transfer to a large serving dish with the meat pieces in the centre. Serve warm.

SYRIA

SERVES 6–8

3 large aubergines
235 ml / 8 fl oz (1 cup) vegetable oil
60 g / 2 oz ($^1/_3$ cup) pine nuts
3 medium onions, peeled and chopped
500 g / 1 lb 2 oz minced beef or lamb
Salt, to taste
$^1/_4$ tsp cinnamon
$^1/_2$ tsp allspice
$^1/_2$ tsp black pepper
1 kg / 2 lb 3 oz tomatoes, peeled and
  chopped
1 Tbsp tomato paste
750 ml / 1$^1/_2$ pints (3 cups) water
2 pitta breads, cut into small pieces
4 garlic cloves, peeled and crushed with
  1 tsp salt
500 ml / 17 fl oz (2 cups) yoghurt

Fattit al makdous
Meat-stuffed aubergines

1 Rinse the aubergines and remove the stalks and caps. Scoop out the aubergine flesh using a scooping tool or a spoon and leaving about 5 mm ($^1/_4$ in) thickness. Rinse and drain.

2 Heat 1 tablespoon vegetable oil in a frying pan. Add the pine nuts and fry over a moderate heat until golden brown. Lift with a slotted spoon. Add half the onion quantity to the same oil and cook until tender. Add the minced meat and stir over a moderate heat until the meat juices have evaporated. Season with salt and the spices. Stir in half the fried pine nuts and remove from the heat.

3 Stuff the aubergines with the meat mixture, then fry them in 4 tablespoons vegetable oil over a moderate heat until lightly browned on all sides. Remove to a plate.

4 To make a tomato sauce, fry the remaining onion in 1 tablespoon vegetable oil until tender. Add the tomatoes and cook over a moderate heat for 10 minutes. Stir in the tomato paste and water, season to taste and bring to the boil. Heat, cover and cook for 10 minutes.

5 Place the aubergines in the pan with the tomato sauce. Cover and simmer for 15 minutes until tender. Fry the bread pieces in hot vegetable oil until browned, then remove to a plate.

6 In a bowl, mix the garlic and salt with the yoghurt. To serve, place the fried bread pieces on a serving dish, top with the aubergines and cover with tomato sauce. Finally, pour over the yoghurt and sprinkle with pine nuts.

EGYPT

SERVES 5–6

1 kg / 2 lb 3 oz minced beef or lamb
2 medium onions, peeled and chopped
90 g / 3 oz (1 cup) parsley, chopped
1 tsp ground cinnamon
1 tsp allspice
1/2 tsp black pepper
1/2 tsp cumin (optional)
2 tsp salt
1 Tbsp vegetable oil
Pitta bread and salad, to serve

Kofta
Minced meat with parsley

1 Place the minced meat, onions, parsley, cinnamon, allspice, black pepper, cumin, if using, and salt in a food processor. Process briefly to a homogeneous paste. Transfer to a bowl, and cover and refrigerate for 2 hours to bring out flavours.

2 Divide the meat mixture into 20 equal portions. Form each portion into fingers about 12 cm (5 in) long. Thread each finger lengthways on a skewer. Grill over glowing charcoal, for about 10 minutes, turning frequently until well done. Remove from the skewers. Serve with pitta bread and salad.

SAUDI ARABIA

SERVES 6

1 kg / 2 lb 3 oz lamb, cubed
3 medium onions, peeled and finely chopped
Salt and black pepper, to taste
1 litre / 1 1/3 pints (4 1/3 cups) water
1/8 tsp cardamom pods
1/8 tsp mastic
500 ml / 17 fl oz (2 cups) milk
400 g / 14 oz (2 cups) basmati or
  long grain rice, rinsed
4 Tbsp melted butter
Green salad, to serve

Saliq
Lamb with milk and rice

1 Place the meat, onions, salt and black pepper in a saucepan. Cover with water and bring to the boil, skimming as necessary. Add the cardamom and mastic. Cover and simmer gently for 1 hour until the meat is tender. Add water if necessary. Remove the meat from the pan and keep warm.

2 Add 470 ml / 16 fl oz (2 cups) water and the milk to the stock in which the meat was cooked and bring to the boil. Stir in the rice, cover and cook gently over a low heat for about 15 minutes, until the rice is just cooked. Turn off the heat and keep covered for 10 minutes to allow to steam. Place the rice on a large serving platter. Arrange the pieces of meat on top. Pour the melted butter over the rice and meat. Serve with a green salad.

Minced meat with parsley

LEBANON

SERVES 4–5

1 kg / 2 lb 3 oz sirloin steak, cut into
  Julienne strips
$^1/_4$ tsp ground mastic
$^1/_8$ tsp of each: ground cardamom,
  ground cloves, ground nutmeg, allspice
  and black pepper
$^1/_4$ tsp cinnamon
2 bay leaves, shredded into small pieces
1 tsp salt
1 lemon peel
60 ml / 2 fl oz ($^1/_4$ cup) lemon juice
60 ml / 2 fl oz ($^1/_4$ cup) white wine vinegar
125 ml / 4 fl oz ($^1/_2$ cup) vegetable oil
3 garlic cloves, peeled and crushed
2 large onions, peeled and sliced
200 g / 7 oz finely minced fat (optional)
5 small tomatoes, halved
Pitta bread, tahini sauce, snipped parsley,
  onion rings and pickles, to serve

 BAHRAIN

SERVES 4

200 g / 7 oz (1 cup) lentils
200 g / 7 oz (1 cup) burghul
  (cracked wheat), soaked in water
  and drained
250 g / 9 oz minced lamb
1 medium onion, peeled and finely chopped
45 g / 1$^1/_2$ oz ($^1/_2$ cup) parsley, chopped
$^1/_2$ tsp salt
$^1/_4$ tsp black pepper
1 tsp marjoram
5 fresh or dried basil leaves, finely chopped
60 g / 2 oz ($^1/_3$ cup) pine nuts

To garnish
1 red pepper, sliced in rings
1 green pepper, sliced in rings
2 Tbsp blanched almonds (optional)

Shawarma
Spiced grilled steaks

1 Place the meat strips in a large bowl. In a small bowl, combine the mastic, cardamom, cloves, nutmeg, allspice, black pepper, cinnamon, bay leaves and salt. Sprinkle the mixed spices over the meat. Add the lemon peel, lemon juice, vinegar, vegetable oil, garlic and onions. Mix well. Cover and marinate overnight in the refrigerator.

2 Preheat the oven to 200° C / 400° F. Place the meat with the marinade in a large baking dish and remove the lemon peel. Add the minced fat if using. Top with the tomatoes. Bake for 30 minutes, until most of the liquid has evaporated, stirring once or twice. Serve with pitta bread, tahini sauce, snipped parsley, onion rings and pickles.

Kibbeh bil adas
Raw meat with cracked wheat and lentils

1 Place the lentils in a saucepan, cover with water and bring to the boil. Cook over a moderate heat until tender, then drain. Combine the lentils and the burghul, then process in a food processor. Set aside.

2 Combine the minced lamb with the onion, parsley, salt, black pepper, marjoram and basil. Process in a food processor to a consistent paste.

3 Add the pine nuts to the lentils and burghul mixture and mix thoroughly. Transfer the mixture to a serving dish. Garnish with green and red peppers and sprinkle with almonds, if desired.

Spiced grilled steaks

YEMEN

SERVES 4

3 Tbsp vegetable oil
2 medium onions, peeled and sliced
500 g / 1 lb 2 oz beef chuck, cut into
   large chunks
3 medium tomatoes, chopped
1 large green pepper, sliced
2 garlic cloves, peeled and crushed
750 ml / 1^1/$_2$ pints (3 cups) water
^{1}/$_2$ Tbsp hawail spices (see page 158)
2 Tbsp fresh coriander, chopped
2 medium carrots, peeled and grated
Boiled white rice, to serve

Lahm al aqda
Beef with tomato sauce

1 Heat the vegetable oil in a large pan. Add the onions and fry over a medium heat for 5 minutes until tender. Add the beef chunks and cook until brown on all sides. Add the tomatoes, green pepper, garlic, water and hawail spices and bring to the boil, then reduce the heat. Cover and simmer gently for 1 hour, until the meat is tender. Add the coriander and carrots and cook for a further 5 minutes. Serve hot with boiled white rice.

 LEBANON

SERVES 4

2 Tbsp corn oil or butter
500 g / 1 lb 2 oz lamb or beef shanks, cubed
Salt and black pepper, to taste
500 ml / 17 fl oz (2 cups) water
6 large onions, peeled and sliced
1 litre / 35 fl oz (4^1/$_3$ cups) yoghurt
1 Tbsp cornflour
1 medium egg white

Laban immou
Meat in yoghurt sauce

1 Heat the corn oil or butter in a saucepan until hot. Add the meat and cook over a medium heat until brown on all sides. Season with salt and black pepper to taste. Add the water to the pan and bring to the boil. Cover and simmer over a low heat for 30 minutes, skimming as necessary. Add the onions and bring to the boil, then reduce the heat. Cover and simmer for a further 30 minutes until the lamb is tender.

2 Meanwhile, place the yoghurt in a bowl and mix with the cornflour and whisked egg white. Strain through a sieve into a heavy-based pan. Place the pan over a medium heat, stirring constantly in one direction with a wooden spoon until the yoghurt starts to boil. Reduce heat and simmer gently, uncovered, for 3 minutes, stirring occasionally.

3 Pour the yoghurt over the meat mixture and gently return to the boil. Simmer for 10 minutes and adjust the seasoning if necessary. Serve hot with boiled white rice.

IRAQ

SERVES 4–6

For the beef shells
400 g / 14 oz (2 cups) short grain or
  regular rice
500 g /1 lb 2 oz lean minced beef
3 Tbsp parsley, finely chopped
Salt and black pepper, to taste

For the stuffing
250 g / 9 oz minced beef
1 medium onion, peeled and finely chopped
1 tsp allspice
1/2 tsp black pepper
Pinch of saffron soaked in 2 Tbsp rose water

For the sauce
2 Tbsp olive oil
4 garlic cloves, peeled and sliced
4 medium tomatoes, peeled and chopped
2 Tbsp tomato paste
Juice of 2 small lemons
1 litre / 35 fl oz (41/3 cups) water
Black pepper and dry mint, to taste

Boiled rice, to serve

Kibbeh hamoud
Kibbeh with lemon

1 Start by preparing the beef shells. Cover the rice with water and soak for 11/2 hours. Drain and process in a food processor until powdery. Add the beef, parsley, salt and black pepper and process for 3 to 4 minutes until all the ingredients are well combined.

2 To make the stuffing, combine the minced beef with the onion, spices and saffron water in a bowl and mix well.

3 Divide the beef shell mixture into 20 to 25 egg-size portions and roll into balls. Make a hole in the ball using your forefinger. Work your finger around the hole pressing gently until you have a thin oval shell of 1/2 cm (1/4 in) thickness. Fill the shell with the stuffing, close and press firmly on both ends and place on a tray.

4 To make the sauce, heat the olive oil in a large saucepan and lightly fry the garlic. Add tomatoes, tomato paste, lemon juice and water and bring to the boil. Gently add the stuffed meat balls one by one. Cover and simmer for 1 hour until well done. Sprinkle with black pepper and dry mint and serve with boiled rice.

The Iraqi national flag

The Saudi Arabian national flag

 IRAQ

SERVES 4–6

12 small lamb shanks
2 medium onions, peeled and finely chopped
60 ml / 2 fl oz (1/4 cup) olive oil
2 garlic cloves, peeled and chopped
1 tsp baharat spices (see page 158)
1/2 tsp turmeric
5 medium tomatoes, peeled and chopped
250 ml / 9 fl oz (1 cup) water
1 Tbsp tomato paste
1 bay leaf
1 dried lime or rind of 1 lemon
Salt and black pepper, to taste
Boiled white rice and salad, to serve

Kouzi ala timman
Lamb shanks with tomato sauce and rice

1 Rinse the lamb shanks in cold water, pat dry and place in an oven-proof dish.

2 In a pan, gently fry the onions in the olive oil until tender. Add the garlic, baharat and turmeric and fry for 1 minute. Add the remaining ingredients and bring to the boil, then simmer over a low heat for 5 minutes.

3 Preheat the oven to 190° C / 375° F. Pour the tomato sauce over the lamb shanks, cover with aluminium foil and cook in the oven for 1 1/2 to 2 hours until the meat is very tender and separates easily from the bone. Arrange the shanks on a bed of boiled white rice, pour over the sauce and serve with salad.

 SAUDI ARABIA

SERVES 5

2 Tbsp olive oil
2 large onions, peeled and chopped
1 kg / 2 lb 3 oz boneless stewing lamb
  or beef, trimmed and cubed
2 tsp baharat spices (see page 158)
2 garlic cloves, peeled and crushed
2 medium tomatoes, peeled and chopped
2 Tbsp tomato paste
2 tsp salt
1/2 tsp ground black pepper
30 g / 1 oz (1/3 cup) parsley, chopped
1 kg / 2 lb 3 oz potatoes, peeled
1 flat bread or pitta bread
Chopped parsley, to garnish
Pickles, to serve

Tharyd
Meat and potato stew

1 Heat the olive oil in a heavy-based saucepan. Add the onions and fry over a moderate heat until tender. Increase the heat and add the meat cubes, stirring frequently for about 20 minutes until all the liquid has evaporated and the meat is brown on all sides. Add the baharat and garlic and cook for 1 minute.

2 Add the tomatoes, tomato paste, salt, black pepper and parsley. Cover and simmer over a low heat for 1 hour. Halve the potatoes if large. Add to the pan, cover and simmer for about 30 minutes until the meat and potatoes are tender.

3 Cut the bread into small pieces and place on a serving dish. Top with the meat, potatoes and sauce and sprinkle with chopped parsley. Serve with pickles.

Lamb shanks with tomato sauce and rice

LEBANON

SERVES 5–6

1 kg / 2 lb 3 oz lean minced beef
1 medium onion, peeled and finely chopped
1 tsp salt
1/2 tsp cinnamon
1/2 tsp allspice
125 ml / 4 fl oz (1/2 cup) vegetable oil
1 kg / 2 lb 3 oz small onions, peeled
2 Tbsp pomegranate molasses or
  juice of 1 lemon
1 litre / 11/3 pint (41/3 cups) water
2 Tbsp plain flour
3 garlic cloves, peeled and crushed
1 tsp dried mint
Boiled rice, to serve

Dawood basha
Meatballs with onion

1 Place the meat, onion, salt and half the spices in food processor bowl. Cover and process shortly to form a homogeneous, firm paste. Roll the meat mixture with wet hands into small walnut-size balls.

2 Heat the vegetable oil in a frying pan until hot. Cook the meatballs in batches over a moderate heat until browned all over. Lift out with a slotted spoon and drain on paper towels.

3 Fry the whole small onions in the same oil until golden brown. Transfer the meatballs and onions to a large saucepan. Add the pomegranate molasses or lemon juice, water and remaining spices to the pan. Bring to the boil, then cover and simmer over a low heat for 30 minutes.

4 Dissolve the flour in 125 ml / 4 fl oz (1/2 cup) cold water. Add to the meat, stirring continuously for 1 minute until the sauce has thickened. Add the garlic and dried mint to the meat and cook for 5 minutes. Serve hot with boiled rice.

 SAUDI ARABIA

SERVES 8

2 kg / 4 lb 6 oz leg of lamb
350 ml / 12 fl oz (11/2 cups) yoghurt
2 Tbsp tomato paste
3 garlic cloves, peeled and chopped
1 tsp of each: black pepper, cardamom,
  cinnamon and cumin
1 tsp saffron
Salt, to taste
125 ml / 4 fl oz (1/2 cup) corn oil
Cooked vegetables and boiled rice, to serve

Fakhtha bel laban
Leg of lamb with yoghurt

1 Trim the leg of lamb and remove the membrane and any excess fat. Slash in several places with a sharp knife.

2 In a bowl, mix the yoghurt with the remaining ingredients. Brush the lamb with this mixture and marinate for 3 hours or overnight in the refrigerator.

3 Preheat the oven to 190° C / 375° F. Place the lamb in a large oven-proof dish and cover with aluminium foil. Keep the marinade for later use. Cook in the oven for 2 to 21/2 hours, basting with the marinade two or three times during the final stages of cooking to prevent drying. Slice and serve with cooked vegetables and boiled rice.

EGYPT

SERVES 5

1 kg / 2 lb 3 oz okra
2 Tbsp ghee or shortening
1 medium onion, peeled and chopped
500 g / 1 lb 2 oz stewing beef or lamb,
  cubed
Salt and black pepper, to taste
500 g / 1 lb 2 oz tomatoes, peeled and
  chopped
235 ml / 8 fl oz (1 cup) water
1 Tbsp tomato paste
3 Tbsp vegetable oil
4 garlic cloves, peeled and crushed
1 Tbsp dried coriander
1 green chilli, chopped (optional)
Juice of 1 lemon
Boiled white rice, to serve

Bamia bi salsat al tamatim

Okra in tomato sauce

1 Trim the okra stems, taking care not to cut through flesh and to keep the cap intact. Rinse, drain and pat dry with kitchen towel. Set aside.

2 Melt 1 tablespoon of the ghee or shortening in a pan, add the onion and cook over a medium heat until tender. Add the meat and brown on all sides. Season with salt and black pepper. Add the tomatoes and cook for about 5 minutes, then stir in the water and the tomato paste. Cover and cook over a moderate heat for 45 minutes until the meat is almost cooked.

3 In a separate pan, fry the okra in the vegetable oil over a moderate heat until slightly browned. Add the okra to the meat pan and cover and cook for 20 minutes.

4 Heat the remaining ghee or shortening in a small pan. Add the garlic, coriander and chilli, if using. Cook, stirring gently until browned. Pour the hot garlic mixture over the okra. Add lemon juice and cook for 10 minutes. Serve hot with boiled white rice.

YEMEN

SERVES 4

1 kg / 2 lb 3 oz beef shanks with bones,
  cut into thick chunks
2 medium onions, peeled and quartered
5 garlic cloves, peeled
3 medium tomatoes, peeled and chopped
Salt and black pepper, to taste
1/2 tsp caraway
1/4 tsp of each: saffron threads, cardamom
  and turmeric
1–2 hot red chilli peppers, chopped
Boiled white rice, to serve

Hore'i

Spiced beef shanks

1 Place the beef chunks in a large saucepan and cover with cold water. Bring to the boil, skimming as necessary. Add the onions, garlic, tomatoes, salt, black pepper and spices. Add 1 or 2 chilli peppers, as desired. Cover and simmer over a low heat for about 1 1/2 hours until the meat is tender and the juice has reduced to a thick sauce. Serve hot with boiled white rice.

CHICKEN

Some of the tastiest Middle-Eastern dishes feature chicken. These range from the inspired simplicity of grilled and roasted preparations to the elaborate dishes cooked with rice or walnuts. The simple yet creative ideas for cooking chicken are as limitless as they are tempting.

In the following pages, you will find flavoursome Chicken kebabs (page 84), marinated in exotic spices and grilled on skewers with mushrooms, and the popular Lebanese Grilled chicken fingers (page 89), marinated in a mixture of garlic, lemon juice and exotic spices, along with a whole host of delectable chicken dishes. These recipes are sure to make your guests happy and coming back for more.

IRAN

SERVES 5

400 g / 14 oz (2 cups) basmati or
   long grain rice
125 ml / 4 fl oz (^{1}/2 cup) vegetable oil
1 large onion, peeled and chopped
Small whole chicken, rinsed and cut
   into 4 pieces
500 ml / 17 fl oz (2 cups) hot water
Salt and black pepper, to season
200 g / 7 oz (1 cup) caster sugar
^{1}/2 tsp saffron
90 g / 3 oz (1 cup) orange peel
2 Tbsp butter
75 g / 2^1/2 oz (^{1}/2 cup) slivered almonds,
   soaked in cold water for 1 hour
75 g /2^1/2 oz (^{1}/2 cup) slivered pistachio nuts

Shirin polow

Chicken with rice and orange peel

1 Rinse the rice twice and soak in warm water for 1 hour.

2 Heat half the quantity of vegetable oil in a pan. Add the onion and fry until slightly browned. Add the chicken pieces and fry until slightly browned. Stir in the hot water, salt and pepper and bring to the boil. Cook over a medium heat for about 20 minutes. Remove the chicken pieces from the pan and remove the bones.

3 Set aside 3 tablespoons sugar for later use. In the same pan, add the remaining sugar to 250 ml / 9 fl oz (1 cup) hot water and bring to the boil. Add 125 ml / 4 fl oz (^{1}/2 cup) chicken stock to the pan with 2 tablespoons oil and the saffron and mix well. Set aside for later use.

4 Thinly slice the orange peel and boil for a few minutes, drain and repeat the process three times. Soak in cold water for 1 hour, then drain. Finally, boil for a few minutes with the reserved sugar and drain.

5 Pour 1.5 litres / 3.2 pints (6^1/4 cups) water in a large non-stick pan and bring to the boil. Add the rice and 2 teaspoons salt. Cook until the rice is slightly soft. Drain and rinse in warm water.

6 Pour 1 tablespoon oil and 1 tablespoon butter into the same pan and add half the rice. Pour another tablespoon oil and the remaining butter over the rice, cover the pan and cook over a low heat for about 30 minutes. Spread the chicken pieces over the rice, and cover with half of the remaining rice. Spread half the almonds and orange peel over the rice and cover with remaining rice. Pour the sugar and reserved chicken stock over the rice. Cover and cook over a low heat for about 30 minutes. Add the remaining almonds, orange peel, and the pistachio nuts and mix well. Transfer to a serving dish and serve immediately.

LEBANON

SERVES 5

1 kg / 2 lb 3 oz chicken breasts, deboned
   and cubed
1 Tbsp ketchup
1 Tbsp tomato paste
1 tsp salt
$^1/_4$ tsp white pepper
4 garlic cloves, peeled and crushed
125 ml / 4 fl oz ($^1/_2$ cup) lemon juice
125 ml / 4 fl oz ($^1/_2$ cup) vegetable oil
1 tsp oregano
2 green peppers, cubed
200 g / 7 oz button mushrooms
Pitta bread and salad, to serve

Shish tawook
Chicken kebabs

1 Mix all the ingredients together in a bowl. Cover and marinate overnight in the refrigerator.

2 Thread the chicken pieces onto skewers, alternating chicken pieces with cubes of green pepper and whole mushrooms. The above quantities will make about 10 skewers.

3 Grill over glowing charcoal for 10 to 12 minutes, turning frequently and brushing with the marinade when required. Alternatively, place in an oven-proof dish and cook in a preheated oven at 190° C / 375° F for 30 minutes until tender. Serve with pitta bread and salad.

 BAHRAIN

SERVES 4–6

Medium whole chicken, cut into 8 pieces
1.5 litres / 3.2 pints (6$^1/_4$ cups) water
3 Tblsp vegetable oil
2 medium onions, peeled and finely chopped
2 garlic cloves, peeled and crushed
1 small piece of fresh ginger, peeled and
   crushed
1 Tbsp tomato paste
2 large potatoes, peeled and cubed
4 courgettes, cubed
2 medium aubergines, cubed
3 medium tomatoes, chopped
2 dried limes or 1 lemon rind
1 small hot green chilli, chopped
1 tsp baharat spices (see page 158)
$^1/_4$ tsp of each: cinnamon, turmeric, curry
   powder, garlic powder, ground coriander,
   cardamom
Pinch of hot chilli powder
1 green pepper, cut into thick slices
90 g / 3 oz (1 cup) fresh coriander, chopped
Boiled rice, to serve

Dajaj salona
Chicken with vegetables

1 Place the chicken pieces in a large pan. Add the water and bring to the boil, skimming as necessary. Cover and cook over a low heat for 25 minutes. Lift the chicken from pan, strain the stock and reserve.

2 Heat the vegetable oil in a large saucepan. Add the onions and cook until golden brown. Stir in the garlic, ginger, tomato paste, potatoes, courgettes, aubergines, tomatoes, dried lime or lemon rind and chilli and cook for 5 minutes.

3 Add the chicken pieces to the pan, along with the reserved stock, baharat spices, all the spices and the green pepper. Bring to the boil, then cover and simmer for 10 minutes. Add the fresh coriander, simmer for a further 10 minutes until the potato and chicken are tender. Serve with boiled rice.

Chicken with vegetables

EGYPT

SERVES 4

For the pigeons
4 small pigeons, with giblets reserved
Salt and black pepper, to season
2 cardamom pods, bruised

For the stuffing
150 g / 5^1/2 oz (^{3}/4 cup) green wheat (freek),
  or rice
1 Tbsp butter
1 medium onion, peeled and finely chopped
4 garlic cloves, peeled and crushed
4 Tbsp fresh coriander, chopped
60 ml / 2 fl oz (^{1}/4 cup) lemon juice
1 small onion, peeled
Salt and black pepper, to season

Parsley sprigs, to garnish

Hamam mishshi bil freek

Wheat-stuffed pigeons

1 Start by preparing the pigeons. Rinse and drain them, then season them inside and out with salt and pepper. Clean and finely chop the livers. Cover and refrigerate until required.

2 To make the stuffing, place the green wheat in a bowl and soak in water for 5 minutes. Strain and squeeze the wheat to extract all the liquid. If using rice instead of green wheat, rinse the rice and drain thoroughly. Heat the butter in a frying pan and gently fry the medium onion until tender. Add the chopped livers and fry until browned on both sides. Add the garlic, coriander, lemon juice, half the small onion and seasoning. Simmer for 3 minutes, stirring occasionally. Stir in the green wheat or rice and cook for 1 minute.

3 Fill the pigeons with the stuffing. Tuck the wings under the body, tie the legs together and close the cavity with a string and thick needle or secure with a toothpick.

4 In a separate pan boil 1.5 litres / 3.2 pints (6^1/4 cups) water. Add the remaining onion, a pinch of salt, the cardamom pods and pigeons to the pan and simmer for 30 to 40 minutes over a low heat until tender.

5 Preheat the oven to 200° C / 400° F. Remove the pigeons from the water, unstring or remove the toothpicks. Transfer them to an oven-proof dish and bake for 30 to 40 minutes until browned. Transfer to a serving dish and garnish with the parsley. Serve hot.

SAUDI ARABIA

SERVES 8

2 medium whole chickens
Salt, to taste
Vegetable oil for frying
6 tomatoes, peeled
125 g / 4^1/2 oz (^{1}/2 cup) yoghurt
1 tsp black pepper
1 tsp ground cumin
3 cinnamon sticks
2 medium onions, peeled and chopped
1 Tbsp olive oil
200 g / 7 oz minced beef
6 medium potatoes, peeled and sliced into
  match-stick size pieces
500 g / 1 lb 2 oz spaghetti
3 hard-boiled eggs, sliced
4 Tbsp parsley, finely chopped

Kousy al-macarona
Spaghetti with chicken

1 Cut each chicken into four pieces. Rinse thoroughly, pat dry and season with salt.

2 Heat 125 ml / 4 fl oz (^{1}/2 cup) vegetable oil in a saucepan. Add the chicken pieces and fry for 5 minutes on each side. Drain some of the oil but keep the chicken in the pan.

3 In a bowl, purée the tomatoes and mix with the yoghurt and half the quantity of spices. Pour this mixture over the chicken and simmer for about 40 minutes, until tender.

4 Cook the onions in the olive oil until tender, then add the minced beef and cook until brown. Season with salt, pepper and the remaining cumin. Set aside.

5 Fry the potatoes in vegetable oil until browned on all sides. Remove from the oil and drain on absorbent paper.

6 Break the spaghetti into medium-sized pieces and cook in hot, salted water until just tender, then drain. Transfer the spaghetti to a serving dish. Arrange the chicken pieces on top and pour over the meat with sauce, potatoes and sliced eggs. Sprinkle with parsley and serve immediately.

 LEBANON

Shawarma dajaj
Grilled chicken fingers

SERVES 5

1 kg / 2 lb 3 oz boned chicken breast, skinned
60 ml / 2 fl oz ($^1/4$ cup) lemon juice
125 ml / 4 fl oz ($^1/2$ cup) vegetable oil
$^1/4$ tsp of each: ground cloves, ground nutmeg, white pepper, allspice
$^1/2$ tsp sumac
$^1/2$ tsp oregano
$^1/8$ tsp ground mastic (optional)
3 garlic cloves, peeled and crushed
2 medium onions, peeled and chopped
Pitta bread, garlic dip, grilled tomatoes, French fries and lettuce leaves, to serve

1 Cut the chicken into Julienne strips. In a bowl, mix the chicken slices with all the other ingredients. Cover and marinate in the refrigerator overnight.

2 Preheat the oven to 200° C / 400° F. Place the chicken with the marinade in an oven-proof dish. Cook in the oven for 20 to 30 minutes until tender. Serve with pitta bread, garlic dip, grilled tomatoes, French fries and lettuce leaves.

Garlic dip: In a bowl, pound 6 peeled garlic cloves with $^1/2$ tsp salt to a smooth paste. In a separate bowl, mix 60 ml / 2 fl oz ($^1/4$ cup) lemon juice and 125 ml / 4 fl oz ($^1/2$ cup) vegetable oil together. Add this gradually to the garlic, blending thoroughly to obtain a homogenous fluid with the consistency of mayonnaise. Mix in 1 tbsp mayonnaise, if required.

SYRIA

SERVES 4–6

6 chicken breasts weighing about 1.5 kg /
  3 lb 5 oz
75 g /2^1/2 oz (^{1}/2 cup) plain flour
60 g / 2 oz (^{1}/4 cup) butter
15 small onions, peeled
5 Tbsp pine nuts
1 litre / 35 fl oz (4 cups) chicken stock
Pinch of salt
^{1}/4 tsp black pepper
^{1}/4 tsp cinnamon
3 Tbsp lemon juice
Parsley sprigs, to garnish
Boiled white rice, to serve

Dajaj ablama
Chicken stew

1 Trim the chicken breasts of any fat, rinse and pat dry. Cut each breast into 3 pieces and dip them in the flour. Melt the butter in a frying pan and fry the chicken pieces over a moderate heat until brown on both sides. Remove the chicken from the pan.

2 Fry the whole onions in the same frying pan until golden brown. Remove then fry the pine nuts until golden brown. Remove and drain on absorbent paper. Add the chicken stock, salt, pepper and cinnamon to the pan, stirring continuously for 2 minutes.

3 Transfer the chicken and onions to a large saucepan. Add the stock and cook over a moderate heat for about 40 minutes until tender. Add the lemon juice and cook for a further 5 minutes. Transfer to a serving dish and garnish with the fried pine nuts and parsley sprigs. Serve with boiled white rice.

 SAUDI ARABIA

SERVES 4

2 chicken breasts weighing about 500 g /
  1 lb 2 oz, skinned and deboned
Salt and black pepper, to taste
1250 ml / 2.6 pints (5 cups) milk
1 tsp ground cardamom
150 g / 5^1/2 oz (^{3}/4 cup) caster sugar
2 Tbsp rose water
2 Tbsp cornflour
^{1}/2 tsp cinnamon

Sidreyat al dajaj
Flavoured chicken breast

1 Place the chicken breasts in a saucepan and cover with cold water. Bring to the boil, skimming as required. Add the salt and pepper to taste, then cover and simmer gently for 40 minutes until well cooked.

2 Chop the chicken breasts into small pieces, then place in a food blender with 1 cup of the milk and the cardamom. Blend thoroughly, then strain through a fine mesh sieve.

3 Place the remaining milk in a pan. Add the sugar and rose water and bring to the boil over a low heat. Stir in the blended chicken. Add the cornflour, stirring constantly until the mixture starts to thicken, then remove from the heat. Pour the mixture into a serving dish and leave aside to set. Sprinkle with the ground cinnamon and place in the refrigerator to cool.

Chicken stew

EGYPT

SERVES 4–6

For the chicken

1.5 kg / 3 lb 5 oz chicken drumsticks, skinned
1/2 tsp black pepper
1 tsp cumin
1/2 tsp ground saffron
1/2 tsp hot red chilli pepper
60 ml / 2 fl oz (1/4 cup) vegetable oil
1 medium onion, peeled and finely chopped
2 tsp cornflour dissolved in 470 ml /
  16 fl oz (2 cups) water
1 cinnamon stick
6 fresh dates, pitted
1 Tbsp lemon juice

For the couscous

500 ml / 17 fl oz (2 cups) chicken stock
1/2 tsp ground saffron
300 g / 101/2 oz (2 cups) couscous
75 g / 21/2 oz whole blanched almonds,
  toasted, to garnish

Tajin al dajaj wil couscous

Chicken with couscous

1 Combine the chicken with the pepper, cumin, saffron and chilli pepper. Cover and marinate for 2 hours in the refrigerator.

2 Heat the vegetable oil in a frying pan and cook the chicken drumsticks until golden brown. Remove from the pan and set aside.

3 Heat the oil again in the same pan, add the onion and cook until transparent. Return the chicken to the pan, stir in the cornflour and cinnamon stick. Cover and simmer gently for 40 minutes until tender.

4 In the meantime, make the saffron couscous. Boil the chicken stock and saffron in a saucepan. Remove from the heat and stir in the couscous. Mix well and let stand for 5 minutes to absorb the liquid.

5 When the chicken is cooked, add the dates and the lemon juice to the pan and cook for a further 5 minutes. Transfer the couscous to a serving dish, place the chicken drumsticks over it and sprinkle with toasted almonds.

UNITED ARAB EMIRATES

SERVES 4–6

Medium whole chicken, cut into 8 pieces
2 litres / 70 fl oz (8 cups) water
2 dried limes or the rind of 1 orange
2 chicken stock cubes
500 g / 1 lb 2 oz (2¹/₂ cups) basmati rice,
  rinsed and drained
2 Tbsp butter
3 medium onions, peeled and sliced
250g / 9 oz (1 cup) yoghurt
1 tsp cornflour
³/₄ tsp of each: black pepper, cumin, fresh
  coriander, turmeric, cardamom and
  cinnamon
3 garlic cloves, peeled and crushed
1 tsp ground saffron soaked in 60 ml /
  2 fl oz (¹/₄ cup) hot water
Fried whole almonds, pine nuts and
  pistachio nuts, to garnish

Dajaj biryani
Chicken biryani

1 Place the chicken pieces and water in a large saucepan. Bring to the boil, skimming whenever necessary. Add the dried limes or orange rind and the chicken stock cubes. Cover and simmer over a low heat for 30 to 40 minutes until tender. Remove the chicken from the stock and set aside.

2 Add the rice to the stock in the pan and cook for 10 minutes until the rice is almost cooked. Drain and set aside.

3 Heat the butter in a large saucepan and fry the onions for 5 to 7 minutes, until golden brown. Stir in the cooked chicken.

4 In a bowl, mix the yoghurt with the cornflour. Strain through a sieve into a heavy-based saucepan. Place the pan over a medium heat, stirring constantly in one direction with a wooden spoon until the yoghurt starts to boil. Reduce the heat and simmer gently, uncovered, for 3 minutes, stirring occasionally. Add all the spices and garlic to the pan. Pour the boiled yoghurt over the chicken. Add half the cooked rice to cover the chicken, then sprinkle with half the saffron water. Add the remaining rice and saffron water. Cover and simmer for 25 to 30 minutes until the rice is tender. Transfer to a large dish and garnish with fried almonds, pine nuts and pistachios.

SAUDI ARABIA

SERVES 4–6

For the chicken
Medium whole chicken
1.5 litres / 3.2 pints (6^1/4 cups) water
2 chicken stock cubes
400 g / 14 oz (2 cups) basmati or
   long grain rice

For the sauce
2 Tbsp vegetable oil
3 medium onions, peeled and finely sliced
125 g / 4^1/2 oz (^{1}/2 cup) yoghurt
4 cardamom pods, bruised
1 Tbsp fresh gingerroot, sliced
1 small cinnamon stick
^{1}/2 tsp of each: black pepper and cumin
   powder
Pinch of ground saffron soaked in 60ml /
   2 fl oz (^{1}/4 cup) of boiling water

Al roz al zerbian
Zerbian chicken

1 Cut the chicken into 8 pieces. Rinse thoroughly and pat dry. Place the chicken pieces, water and stock cubes in a large saucepan. Bring to the boil, skimming as necessary. Cover and leave to simmer over a low heat for 45 minutes until tender.

2 Remove the chicken from the stock and set aside. Add the rice to the pan and bring to the boil. Simmer over a medium heat for 10 minutes until the rice is half cooked, then drain.

3 To make the sauce, heat the vegetable oil in a medium-size saucepan. Add the onions and fry for 6 to 8 minutes until golden brown. In a large bowl, mix the yoghurt with all the spices. Carefully add the chicken to the yoghurt mixture, and pour this mixture over the onions in the saucepan. Pour the semi-cooked rice over the chicken mixture. Sprinkle with saffron water. Cover and simmer over a low heat for 25 minutes until the rice is cooked. Transfer the rice and chicken to a serving dish and serve immediately.

IRAN

SERVES 4

3 Tbsp vegetable oil
2 large onions, peeled and finely chopped
2 tsp turmeric powder
1/2 tsp black pepper
1 tsp lime powder or orange rind
Pinch of saffron
1 kg / 2 lb 3 oz chicken pieces with bones
3 Tbsp tomato paste
1200 ml / 2 pints (5 cups) water
200 g / 7 oz (1 cup) dried split chickpeas
Boiled rice, to serve

Gheymeh
Chicken with chickpeas

1 Heat the vegetable oil in a large saucepan and fry the onions for 4 to 5 minutes until tender. Add the turmeric powder, pepper, lime powder, saffron and chicken pieces to the pan, stirring for 3 to 4 minutes. Add the tomato paste and stir for 1 to 2 minutes.

2 Add in the water and bring to the boil, then reduce the heat. Cover and simmer for 20 minutes until the chicken is half-way cooked. Add the chickpeas and simmer for 45 minutes until the chicken and chickpeas are tender. Add more water if necessary. Serve with boiled rice.

 IRAQ

SERVES 4–6

Medium whole chicken
1 lemon, halved
Salt and black pepper, to taste
2 Tbsp vegetable oil
10 garlic cloves, left whole and unpeeled
Juice of 1 lemon
1 litre / 35 fl oz (4 cups) water
4 medium potatoes, peeled and cubed
1 Tbsp cornflour
Boiled white rice, to serve

Tashreeb dajaj
Pot roasted chicken

1 Rinse the chicken, drain and pat dry. Rub it with the lemon halves, then season with salt and pepper and refrigerate for 30 minutes.

2 Heat the vegetable oil in a saucepan and cook the whole chicken until browned on all sides. Remove the outer layers of the garlic cloves but leave them unpeeled. Rinse and add to the chicken along with the lemon juice and water. Cover and simmer gently over a low heat for 45 minutes. Add the potatoes and simmer for a further 15 minutes.

3 When tender, transfer the chicken to a platter and keep hot. Remove the garlic, keeping four cloves and discard the rest. Add the cornflour to the juices and reduce over a high heat to 470 ml / 16 fl oz (2 cups). Peel the four garlic cloves, crush them and mix with the juices, adjusting the seasoning to taste. Cut the chicken into serving portions and pour the juices over the chicken. Serve hot with boiled white rice.

LEBANON

SERVES 5

Medium whole chicken, skinned and
 cut into 8 pieces
1 tsp salt
60 g / 2 oz (1/4 cup) butter or
 60 ml / 2 fl oz (1/4 cup) corn oil
1.5 litres / 3.2 pints (6 1/4 cups) hot water
1 cinnamon stick
1 small onion, peeled
1 parsley sprig
1 bay leaf
1/2 tsp of each: allspice, cinnamon powder
 and black pepper
250 g / 9 oz minced beef or lamb
2 Tbsp butter
400 g / 14 oz (2 cups) long grain rice
5 Tbsp blanched almonds
5 Tbsp pine nuts

Djaj bel rouz
Chicken and rice

1 Rinse the chicken, drain and rub it with the salt.

2 Heat the butter or corn oil in a frying pan. Add the chicken pieces and brown on both sides. Transfer the chicken pieces to a deep pan, cover with the hot water and bring to the boil, skimming as necessary. Add the cinnamon stick, whole onion, parsley sprig, bay leaf, half the spices and a pinch of salt. Cover and simmer over a low heat for 45 minutes.

3 In another pan, fry the minced meat in 1 tablespoon butter until browned. Season with salt and the remainder of the spices. Add the rice, stirring for 2 minutes.

4 Measure 1 litre / 35 fl oz (4 cups) of the chicken stock from Step 2 and strain into the rice and meat pan. Bring to the boil, then cover and simmer gently for 30 to 40 until the rice is tender, stirring once or twice during cooking.

5 Brown the almonds and pine nuts in 1 tablespoon butter and set aside. Pour the rice onto a large platter, top with the chicken pieces and sprinkle with almonds and pine nuts.

SAUDI ARABIA

SERVES 4–6

Medium whole chicken
125 ml / 4 fl oz (¹/2 cup) corn oil
2 onions, peeled and finely chopped
¹/2 Tbsp of each: ground coriander, black
  pepper and salt
1 red chilli pepper
500 ml / 17 fl oz (2 cups) yoghurt
250 ml / 9 fl oz (1 cup) water
1 tsp cornflour
1 egg white
Boiled white rice, to serve

Dajaj bel laban
Chicken with yoghurt

1 Rinse the chicken, remove the skin and cut into 8 pieces. Heat the corn oil in a saucepan and fry the onions until tender. Add the chicken pieces and brown on both sides. Add the ground coriander, pepper, salt and chilli pepper. Cook over a low heat for 45 minutes, stirring occasionally and adding small amounts of water as required.

2 Place the yoghurt in a bowl and mix it with the water, cornflour and egg white. Strain through a sieve into a heavy-based pan. Place the pan over a medium heat, stirring constantly in one direction with a wooden spoon until it starts to boil. Reduce the heat and simmer gently, uncovered, for 3 minutes, stirring occasionally.

3 When the chicken is cooked, add the yoghurt mixture and continue to simmer over a low heat for 15 minutes. Serve in a deep dish with boiled white rice.

SAUDI ARABIA

SERVES 4–5

Medium whole chicken, rinsed and
  cut into 8 pieces
1 cinnamon stick
2 cloves
3 black peppercorns
2 cardamom pods, bruised
1 bay leaf
1 fresh coriander sprig
1 onion, peeled and quartered
500 ml / 17 fl oz (2 cups) milk
400 g / 14 oz (2 cups) long grain rice, rinsed
3 Tbsp melted butter

Saliq dajaj
Chicken with milk and rice

1 Place the chicken pieces in a pot, cover with water and bring to the boil, skimming as necessary. Add the cinnamon stick, cloves, peppercorns, cardamom pods, bay leaf, coriander sprig and onion. Cover and simmer over a low heat for 45 minutes, until the chicken is tender.

2 Lift out the chicken and set aside. Add the milk and rice to the chicken stock and cook for 10 minutes until the rice is just tender.

3 Remove the bones from the chicken and cut into small pieces. Add the pieces to the rice and cook gently for 10 minutes, stirring once or twice. Place in a serving dish and drizzle with the melted butter.

Chicken with yoghurt

KUWAIT

SERVES 6

Medium whole chicken
Salt and black pepper, to season
400 g / 14 fl oz (2 cups) long grain rice
60 ml / 2 fl oz (¹/4 cup) vegetable oil
2 medium onions, peeled and sliced
350 g / 12¹/2 oz tomato purée
2 medium tomatoes, chopped
4 garlic cloves, peeled and crushed
1.5 litres / 3.2 pints (6¹/4 cups) hot water
2 medium carrots, peeled and grated
Grated rind of 1 orange
4 cloves
4 cardamom pods
3 cinnamon sticks
4 Tbsp raisins
4 Tbsp slivered almonds

Kabsat al dajaj

Chicken with rice and tomatoes

1 Cut the chicken into 8 pieces. Rinse thoroughly, then pat dry and season with salt and pepper. Thoroughly rinse the rice and soak in salted water for about 30 minutes.

2 Heat the vegetable oil in a large saucepan. Add the onions and fry until golden brown. Add the chicken pieces, tomato purée, chopped tomatoes and garlic stirring for about 5 minutes over a low heat.

3 Stir in the hot water, grated carrots, orange rind, spices, and salt and pepper, to taste. Cover and cook over a medium heat for 40 minutes until the chicken is tender. Remove the chicken and keep in a warm place.

4 Add the rice to the liquid in the saucepan, cover and simmer for about 35 minutes until all the liquid has absorbed and rice is tender. Transfer the rice to the centre of a serving platter and arrange the chicken pieces around it. Top with the raisins and almonds.

SYRIA

SERVES 4–6

300 g / 10¹/2 oz (1¹/2 cups) dry chickpeas
1 tsp bicarbonate of soda
Medium whole chicken, skinned and
   cut into 4 pieces
700 ml / 1 pint (3 cups) water
¹/2 tsp of each: black pepper, cinnamon
   and allspice
8 small onions, peeled and left whole
1 tsp salt
300 g / 10¹/2 oz (2 cups) coarse burghul
   (coarse cracked wheat)
3 Tbsp butter or corn oil
Yoghurt or salad, to serve

Burghul bi dfeen

Cracked wheat with chicken

1 Place the chickpeas in a bowl and cover with water. Add the bicarbonate of soda to the water and soak the chickpeas overnight. Drain the chickpeas and rinse under running water.

2 Place the chickpeas in a pan or a pressure cooker, cover with water and bring to the boil. Cook over a low heat for 30 to 45 minutes until half cooked.

3 Place the chicken pieces in another pan, cover with the water and bring to the boil, skimming as necessary. Cook for 5 minutes. Transfer the chicken to the chickpea pan, add all the spices, onions and salt. Cover and cook for 20 to 30 minutes over a low heat until both the chicken pieces and chickpeas are tender.

4 Thoroughly rinse the burghul and add it to the pan. If using a pressure cooker, do not close the lid firmly at this stage. Cook gently for 15 minutes until most of the liquid has been absorbed. Stir in the butter and cook for a further 5 minutes. Adjust seasoning. Serve hot with yoghurt or salad.

KUWAIT

SERVES 4–5

Medium whole chicken
2 Tbsp ghee or shortening
2 large onions, peeled and chopped
1 Tbsp baharat spices (see page 158)
1 tsp turmeric
3 medium tomatoes, peeled and chopped
1/4 tsp cloves
1/2 tsp dried lime
2 cinnamon sticks
6 cardamom pods, bruised
3 tsp salt
950 ml / 32 fl oz (4 cups) water
400 g / 14 oz (2 cups) basmati or
  long grain rice
2 Tbsp parsley, chopped
2 Tbsp fresh coriander, chopped

Machbous ala dajaj

Spiced chicken with rice

1 Cut the chicken into 8 pieces. Rinse thoroughly and pat dry.

2 Heat the ghee or shortening in a deep, heavy-based saucepan. Gently fry the onions until transparent and slightly brown. Stir in the baharat spices and turmeric and cook for a further 2 minutes.

3 Stir in the chicken pieces and cook over a medium heat until light brown. Add tomatoes, cloves, dried lime, cinnamon sticks, cardamom pods and salt, stirring well. Then add the water, cover and simmer gently for 30 to 40 minutes.

4 Place the rice in a bowl and rinse with cold water until the water runs clear, then drain. Gently stir the rice into the saucepan, add the herbs and bring back to a slow simmer. If necessary add hot water to cover the rice and chicken. Cover and simmer over a low heat for 30 minutes until the rice is tender, stirring gently once or twice during cooking. Remove from the heat and set aside to rest for 10 minutes. Transfer the rice to a large serving platter and place the chicken pieces over the rice. Serve hot.

IRAN

SERVES 6

Medium whole chicken, cut into 8 pieces
125 ml / 4 fl oz ($^1/_2$ cup) vegetable oil
3 medium onions, peeled and thinly sliced
1.5 litres / 3.2 pints (6$^1/_4$ cups) hot water
500 g / 1 lb 2 oz fresh herbs (parsley, mint,
  fresh coriander and green onion)
2 garlic cloves, peeled and crushed
Salt, to taste
500 g / 1 lb 2 oz ground walnuts
2 Tbsp caster sugar
500 ml / 17 fl oz (2 cups) fresh pomegranate
  juice, or 60 ml / 2 fl oz ($^1/_4$ cup)
  pomegranate molasses
1 tsp cornflour
1 Tbsp walnuts, halved, to garnish
Boiled white rice, to serve

Khoesht anaar-aveej
Chicken with walnuts and herbs

1 Rinse the chicken pieces, drain and pat dry. Heat the vegetable oil in a large saucepan. Add the onions and cook until tender. Add chicken pieces and cook until the colour changes. Add the hot water and bring to the boil. Reduce the heat and simmer slowly for about 10 minutes.

2 Rinse and finely chop the herbs. In a separate pan, fry the herbs with the garlic in 1 tablespoon vegetable oil until tender, for about 3 minutes. Transfer the herbs and garlic to the chicken pan and add the salt, ground walnuts, sugar and pomegranate juice or molasses. Simmer for about 1 hour until the oil in the walnuts is released and sauce starts to thicken.

3 Dissolve the cornflour in 60 ml / 2 fl oz ($^1/_4$ cup) cold water and add to the chicken, stirring for 2 minutes. Remove from the heat and pour the chicken with the sauce into a serving platter and garnish with the walnuts. Serve hot with boiled white rice.

JORDAN

SERVES 2

Medium whole chicken
Salt, to taste
1/2 tsp allspice
1/2 tsp black pepper
125 ml / 4 fl oz (1/2 cup) olive oil
6 medium onions, peeled and sliced
3 Tbsp sumac
2 pitta bread (or thin flat bread)

Musakhan

Chicken roasted with bread

1 Clean the chicken and cut into two halves. Season with the salt, allspice and pepper.

2 Heat half the olive oil in a large frying pan. Fry the two chicken pieces over a medium heat until lightly browned on both sides. Transfer to a plate and set aside.

3 Add remaining olive oil to the pan with the onions. Fry gently, stirring often, until the onions are tender. Add the sumac and cook for 2 minutes, then remove from the heat.

4 Preheat the oven to 190° C / 375° F. Split the pitta bread into two parts and place in the base of a baking dish. Spread half the fried onions in the centre of each pitta bread half. Top each mound with a chicken half and spread the remaining onion mixture over each chicken half. Pour the oil from the pan over chicken. Cover the chicken completely with the remaining bread and sprinkle the bread with water.

5 Bake for 40 minutes, or until the chicken is tender and cooked through. When the bread begins to brown, sprinkle again lightly with water or cover the baking dish with a piece of aluminium foil. Serve hot.

FISH

For centuries, the inhabitants of the coastal areas surrounding the Mediterranean and the Gulf relied heavily on the bounty of the sea, and so fish played an important part in their diet. Today, fresh fish and seafood are a favourite choice because they are healthy, high in protein, low in fat and are a great source of essential vitamins.

The fish recipes in this section are succulent whether grilled, baked, fried, stuffed, minced or prepared as a stew. You will find Sayyadiah (page 112), the delicately spiced fish served on a bed of rice, and Samke harrah (page 118), spicy fish lightly fried and baked in tahini sauce, in addition to many other mouthwatering recipes. No matter what your choice is, the fish should always be fresh.

LEBANON

SERVES 4–5

For the fish
1 kg / 2 lb 3 oz white fish fillet,
  such as snapper, grouper, cod or hake
4 Tbsp olive oil
4 medium onions, peeled and chopped
5 garlic cloves, peeled and crushed
90 g / 3 oz (1 cup) fresh coriander, chopped
2 medium tomatoes, chopped
1 hot chilli, chopped
1 Tbsp tomato paste
125 g / 4 oz (1 cup) walnuts, chopped
2 Tbsp pine nuts

For the sauce
60 ml / 2 fl oz ($^1/4$ cup) tahini
60 ml / 2 fl oz ($^1/4$ cup) lemon juice
60 ml / 2 fl oz ($^1/4$ cup) water
Salt and black pepper, to taste
Bread, to serve

Samak bi taratour
Fish with tahini sauce and walnuts

1 Preheat the oven to 200° C / 400° F. Start by preparing the fish. Rinse the fillets and pat dry with kitchen paper. Place them in a greased oven-proof dish and cook in the oven for about 25 minutes, until tender.

2 Heat 2 tablespoons olive oil in a frying pan and fry the onions until golden brown. Add the garlic, coriander, tomatoes, chilli and tomato paste. Bring to the boil for 2 minutes, then remove from heat.

3 To make the tahini sauce, combine all the sauce ingredients together. Add the sauce to the pan with the onion mixture and return to the heat, stirring continuously until it starts to boil. Remove from heat.

4 In a separate frying pan, brown the walnuts in 2 tablespoons olive oil, then remove from the heat. Add the pine nuts to the oil and brown.

5 To serve, place the fish fillet on a platter, top with the tahini sauce and garnish with the walnuts and pine nuts. Serve with bread.

LEBANON

SERVES 6

1.5 kg / 3 lb 5 oz red snapper or any other
  large fish, such as sea bream, hake or cod
1/2 tsp salt
250 ml / 9 fl oz (1 cup) olive oil
7 medium onions, peeled and sliced
  lengthways
1 tsp black pepper
1 Tbsp cumin
1 litre / 35 fl oz (4 cups) hot water
Juice of 2 lemons
2 Tbsp pomegranate molasses
600 g / 1 lb 5 oz (3 cups) long grain rice,
  rinsed and drained
75 g / 2 1/2 oz (1/2 cup) pine nuts
75 g / 2 1/2 oz (1/2 cup) whole almonds,
  blanched
2 Tbsp vegetable oil

Sayyadiah
Fish with rice

1 Scale, clean and rinse the fish. Pat it dry with paper towels and sprinkle the surface and cavities with the salt. Cover and refrigerate for 30 minutes.

2 Heat the olive oil in a deep pan. Brown the fish over a high heat, for about 7 minutes on each side. Remove from the heat, then remove the fish bones, skin and heads (but save the heads). Cut the fish into serving pieces and set aside.

3 Fry the onions in the same oil over a low heat, for about 15 minutes, until golden brown. Remove half the onions and set aside for garnishing. Continue cooking the remaining onions for another 5 minutes until dark brown. Add the fish heads, pepper, cumin and hot water. Cover and simmer gently for 30 minutes. Then discard the fish heads. Stir the onion mixture well, then add the lemon juice and pomegranate molasses. Heat until boiling.

4 Add the rice to the onion mixture pan, cover and cook over a low heat for 25 to 30 minutes until tender. Add more hot water if needed.

5 Brown the pine nuts and almonds in the vegetable oil. Lift and drain on absorbent paper. Pour the rice on a serving dish. Top with the fish pieces and sprinkle with the reserved onions, pine nuts and almonds. Serve hot.

KUWAIT

SERVES 4–5

For the prawn paste
1 kg / 2 lb 3 oz raw prawns, shelled
  and deveined
200 g / 7 oz (1 cup) ground rice
3 Tbsp fresh coriander, chopped
1/2 tsp turmeric
1/2 tsp salt

For the stuffing
1 Tbsp butter
2 medium onions, peeled and chopped
200 g / 7 oz raw prawns, shelled and
  chopped
1 tsp baharat spices (see page 158)
1 tsp dried lime or grated rind of 1 lemon
1/2 tsp salt
2 Tbsp raisins

For the sauce
1 Tbsp butter
2 medium onions, peeled and chopped
2 garlic cloves, peeled and crushed
2 Tbsp fresh coriander, chopped
2 medium tomatoes, peeled and chopped
1 tsp baharat spices (see page 158)
1/2 tsp salt
2 Tbsp tamarind, soaked in 470 ml / 16 fl oz
  (2 cups) warm water

Boiled white rice, to serve

Kebab al rubyan
Prawn balls

1 Start by preparing the prawn paste. Rinse and dry the prawns. Using a food processor, process the prawns with ground rice, coriander, turmeric and salt until thoroughly blended. Cover and refrigerate for 30 minutes.

2 To make the stuffing, melt the butter in a pan and gently fry onions until tender. Add the chopped prawns, baharat spices, dried lime or lemon rind, salt and raisins. Cook until the prawn pieces are tender. Remove from heat and set aside.

3 To make the tamarind sauce, melt the butter in a pan and gently fry onions and garlic until tender. Add the coriander, tomatoes, baharat spices and salt and cook for 2 minutes. Strain the tamarind liquid and add it to the sauce. Cover and simmer gently for 20 minutes.

4 In the meantime, prepare the prawn balls. Take a piece of prawn paste the size of an egg and flatten with moistened hands to a 10-cm (4-in) patty. Place a tablespoon of stuffing in the centre of the patty, then close it up, shaping it into a ball. Repeat with the remaining ingredients.

5 Gently drop the prawn balls into the simmering tamarind sauce. Cover and simmer for 30 minutes. When cooked, remove the balls from the sauce with a slotted spoon and serve hot on a bed of white rice. Pour some of the sauce over the rice.

UNITED ARAB EMIRATES

SERVES 5

75 g / 2^1/2 oz (^{1}/2 cup) plain flour
^{1}/4 tsp salt
Pinch of black pepper
1 kg / 2 lb 3 oz hamour fish or
  white fish fillets
125 ml / 4 fl oz (^{1}/2 cup) olive oil
2 medium onions, peeled and thinly sliced
1 green pepper, cut into long thin strips
2 Tbsp parsley
Lemon wedges, to garnish
Baked potatoes, to serve

Samak bil khidar
Fried fish with vegetables

1 Combine the flour, salt and pepper. Dip the fish fillets in the flour mixture to coat lightly.

2 Heat half the quantity of olive oil in a large frying pan. Add the fish and fry until tender and browned on both sides, for about 10 minutes, then remove and place on a platter. Keep warm.

3 Pour the remaining olive oil into the frying pan. Add the onions, green pepper and parsley. Cook until the onions are tender and season with salt and pepper to taste. Spoon the onion mixture over the fish and garnish with lemon wedges. Serve hot with baked potatoes.

 SAUDI ARABIA

SERVES 5–6

1 kg / 2 lb 3 oz raw shrimps, shelled and
  deveined
Pinch of salt
1 Tbsp plain four
400 g / 14 oz (2 cups) rice
1 litre / 35 fl oz (4 cups) hot water
235 ml / 8 fl oz (1 cup) tomato juice
^{1}/2 tsp each of cinnamon, cardamom and
  black pepper
Salt, to taste
60 ml / 2 fl oz (^{1}/4 cup) corn oil
2 medium onions, peeled and chopped

Roz bel jamberry
Rice with shrimps

1 Thoroughly rinse the shrimps and rub with the salt and flour. Set aside.

2 Thoroughly rinse the rice. Cook in a saucepan with the hot water, tomato juice, all the spices and salt, to taste, over a low heat for about 25 minutes until tender.

3 Heat the corn oil in a frying pan and fry the onions until golden brown. Add the shrimps and cook for 3 minutes on each side. Add the cooked rice to the shrimps and simmer over a low heat for 5 minutes. Serve hot.

Fried fish with vegetables

LEBANON

SERVES 5

1 large snapper or grouper fish weighing
   about 2 kg / 4 lb 6 oz
1/2 tsp salt
125 ml / 4 fl oz (1/2 cup) vegetable oil
10 garlic cloves, peeled
45 g / 1 1/2 oz (1/2 cup) fresh coriander,
   finely chopped
1 Tbsp dried ground coriander
1 hot red chilli, chopped
250 ml / 9 fl oz (1 cup) tahini
500 ml / 17 fl oz (2 cups) cold water
180 ml / 6 fl oz (3/4 cup) lemon juice
4 Tbsp pine nuts

Samke harrah

Spicy fish

1 Clean and scale the fish. Rub it with the salt, then cover and refrigerate for 2 hours.

2 Heat the vegetable oil in a large frying pan. Add the fish and fry over a high heat for 3 to 4 minutes on each side. Carefully transfer the fish to an oven-proof dish along with 2 tablespoons of the frying oil.

3 Preheat the oven to 200° C / 400° F. In a small bowl, crush the garlic cloves with 1/2 teaspoon salt. Mix with the fresh and ground coriander and half the chilli. Stuff the fish cavity with half the garlic mixture.

4 Place the tahini in a small bowl, then gradually add the water, beating continuously. Stir in the lemon juice and the remaining garlic mixture. Pour the sauce over the fish. If the sauce doesn't cover the fish completely, add a little more water. Cook in the oven for 20 to 25 minutes until the fish is tender and the sauce is bubbling.

5 In the meantime, heat 1 tablespoon vegetable oil in a small frying pan and fry the pine nuts until golden brown. Carefully transfer the fish to a platter. Top with the cooking juices and sprinkle with the pine nuts. Serve hot.

EGYPT

SERVES 5

1 kg / 2 lb 3 oz fresh sardines
5 garlic cloves, peeled
1 Tbsp salt
1/4 tsp black pepper
1/2 tsp cumin
250 ml / 9 fl oz (1 cup) lemon juice
1 hot red chilli pepper
180 ml / 6 fl oz (3/4 cup) vegetable oil
3 medium tomatoes, sliced into thick rings
2 green peppers, sliced into thin rings
3 lemons, sliced into rings

Sardine bil forn

Baked sardines

1 Remove the guts and head of the sardines. Rinse thoroughly, then drain.

2 Crush the garlic with the salt. Stir in the pepper, cumin, lemon juice and chilli. Marinate the sardines in this mixture for 1 hour.

3 Preheat the oven to 190° C / 375° F. Transfer the fish with marinade to a baking dish and pour over the vegetable oil. Top with the tomatoes, the green peppers and the lemon slices.

4 Cook in the oven for 30 to 40 minutes, until the fish is cooked and golden brown. Serve hot or cold with tahini sauce.

YEMEN

SERVES 5–6

1 kg / 2 lb 3 oz white fish fillet, such as cod, hake or hamour, cut into serving pieces
4 Tbsp fresh coriander, chopped
2 Tbsp fresh dill, chopped
4 Tbsp vegetable oil
1 Tbsp salt
2 medium onions, peeled and thinly sliced
1 green chilli, chopped
3 medium tomatoes, chopped
240 ml / 8 fl oz (1 cup) hot water
1/2 tsp of each: allspice, cumin, black pepper and cardamom
Boiled white rice, to serve

Matfiya

Fried fish with onion and tomato

1 In a bowl, combine the fish fillet with 2 tablespoons coriander, the dill, 1 tablespoon vegetable oil and salt. Cover and marinate for 1 hour in the refrigerator.

2 Heat the remaining oil in a large frying pan. Add the fish, stirring frequently for about 6 minutes, until golden brown.

3 Add the onions, chilli and tomatoes to the pan and cook for a further 8 minutes. Stir in the hot water with the remaining coriander and all the spices. Bring to the boil, then reduce the heat and simmer for 10 minutes. Serve hot with boiled white rice.

Baked sardines

UNITED ARAB EMIRATES

SERVES 4

1 kg / 2 lb 3 oz shrimps, shelled
  and deveined
Salt, to taste
3 Tbsp plain flour
2 Tbsp butter
2 tsp olive oil
1 large onion, peeled and chopped
3 garlic cloves, peeled and crushed
3 Tbsp fresh coriander, chopped
Juice of 1 lemon
Coriander sprigs, to garnish
Boiled rice and sautéed vegetables, to serve

 EGYPT

SERVES 4–5

1 kg / 2 lb 3 oz hamour or white fish fillet,
  such as cod or flounder
Juice of 1 lemon
Pinch of salt
$1/4$ tsp black pepper
$1/4$ tsp allspice
125 ml / 4 fl oz ($1/2$ cup) corn oil
5 medium onions, peeled and sliced
500 ml / 17 fl oz (2 cups) tomato juice
5 garlic cloves, peeled and chopped
2 Tbsp coriander powder
Salt, to taste
250 ml / 9 fl oz (1 cup) water
3 Tbsp plain flour

Rubyan
Garlic shrimps

1 Sprinkle the shrimps with salt, then dip them in flour to coat.

2 Melt the butter and olive oil in a large frying pan. Add the onion and garlic and cook until tender. Add the shrimps and coriander. Cook, stirring regularly, until the shrimps are golden brown, for about 5 minutes.

3 Transfer the shrimps to a platter, sprinkle with the lemon juice and garnish with sprigs of coriander. Serve hot with boiled rice and sautéed vegetables.

Kozbariet al samak
Fish fillet with coriander

1 Rinse the fish and pat it dry with paper towels. In a bowl, mix the lemon juice, salt, pepper and allspice. Place the fillets in the bowl and toss gently until well coated. Cover and refrigerate for 2 hours.

2 Heat 2 tablespoons corn oil in a frying pan. Add the onions and cook until tender. Stir in the tomato juice, garlic, coriander, salt and water. Bring to the boil, then reduce the heat. Simmer gently for 20 minutes until sauce has thickened.

3 Preheat the oven to 200° C / 400° F. Dip the fillets in the flour to coat them and fry in hot corn oil until lightly browned on both sides. Spread half the quantity of tomato sauce in a 30-cm (12-in) oven-proof dish. Arrange the fish fillets on top, then pour the remaining tomato sauce over the top. Cook in the oven for 30 minutes until golden brown. Serve hot.

EGYPT

SERVES 5

1 kg / 2 lb 3 oz seabass fillet, sliced
  into 5 pieces
1 tbsp salt
1/4 tsp black pepper
1/4 tsp cumin
Juice of 2 lemons
125 ml / 4 fl oz (1/2 cup) corn oil
75 g / 2 1/2 oz (1/2 cup) plain flour
3 medium onions, peeled and chopped
3 green peppers, coarsely chopped
4 garlic cloves, peeled and crushed
500 ml / 17 fl oz (2 cups) fresh tomato juice
1 Tbsp tomato paste
1/2 tsp dried coriander
90 g / 3 oz (1 cup) fresh coriander, chopped
45 g / 1 1/2 oz (1/2 cup) dill, chopped
2 medium tomatoes, thickly sliced
Boiled, buttered rice, to serve

Tagin samak
Baked fish

1 Place the fish slices in a bowl. Add the salt, pepper, half the cumin, lemon juice, 4 tablespoons of the corn oil and the flour. Toss gently to coat the fish pieces. Cover and marinate for 2 hours.

2 Preheat the oven to 190° C / 375° F. Transfer the fish pieces with the marinade to an oven-proof dish. Cover and cook in the oven for 10 minutes.

3 Heat the remaining corn oil in a frying pan. Stir in the onions, green peppers and garlic and cook for 5 minutes. Before the vegetables start browning, add the tomato juice, tomato paste, remaining cumin and dried coriander and cook for a further 5 minutes over a medium heat. Add the fresh coriander and dill and cook for 1 minute.

4 Divide the mixture into two equal portions. Evenly spread one portion of the mixture in an oven-proof dish. Add a layer of part-cooked fish and cover with a second portion of the mixture, then top with tomato slices. Cook in the oven for 15 minutes. Serve with boiled, buttered rice.

LEBANON

SERVES 3–4

10–12 red mullets
1 Tbsp salt
3 Tbsp plain flour
250 ml / 9 fl oz (1 cup) vegetable oil,
  for deep frying
Baked potatoes, salad and bread, to serve

Sultan Ibrahim Mikli
Fried red mullet

1 Clean and scale the fish. Rinse and thoroughly drain. Rub the fish inside and out with the salt. Cover and refrigerate for 1 hour so that fish absorbs the salt.

2 Sprinkle the fish with the flour. Heat the vegetable oil in a frying pan and fry the fish over a high heat for 5 to 7 minutes on each side, until tender and golden brown. Carefully lift the fish out of the pan and drain on absorbent paper. Serve warm with baked potatoes, salad and bread.

KUWAIT

SERVES 4–5

2 Tbsp vegetable oil
1 kg / 2 lb 3 oz raw shrimps, shelled and
  deveined
4 garlic cloves, peeled and crushed
1 medium onion, peeled and chopped
1 tsp baharat spices (see page 158)
Pinch of ground hot red chilli
1 tsp turmeric
1 Tbsp parsley, chopped
2 Tbsp fresh coriander, chopped
2 medium tomatoes, peeled and chopped
2 tsp salt
Black pepper, to taste
500 ml / 17 fl oz (2 cups) water
400 g / 14 oz (2 cups) basmati or
  long grain rice
Salad, to serve

Machbous ala rubyan

Spiced shrimps

1 In a large saucepan, heat the vegetable oil and add the shrimps and garlic. Fry over a moderate heat until the shrimps turn pink, for about 2 minutes on each side. Remove from the heat and set side.

2 Stir in the onion and cook gently until tender and browned. Season with the baharat spices, chilli and turmeric.

3 Add the parsley, coriander, tomatoes, salt, pepper and water. Bring to the boil, then cover and cook over a moderate heat for 3 to 4 minutes.

4 Rinse the rice until the water runs clear. Add it to the saucepan, bring to the boil, then cover and cook for 12 minutes. Add more water if necessary. Add the shrimps to the rice, stirring lightly. Cover and simmer gently over a low heat for 20 minutes. Stir, remove from the heat and leave covered for 5 minutes. Transfer to a serving dish. Serve hot with salad.

IRAQ

SERVES 6

1 whole perch, trout or carp weighing
 about 1.5 kg / 3 lb 5 oz
4 Tbsp vegetable oil
3 large onions, peeled and thinly sliced
5 garlic cloves, peeled and crushed
1 tsp curry powder
1 tsp ground dried lime or
 grated rind of 1 lemon
2 tsp salt
2 Tbsp tamarind paste
250 ml / 9 fl oz (1 cup) warm water
3 Tbsp parsley, chopped
3 Tbsp fresh coriander, chopped
Green salad, to serve

Samak mishwi

Oven barbecued fish

1 Clean and scale the fish. Cut it open lengthways from the head to the tail through the back. Rinse and pat dry with paper towels. Place the fish under the grill for 5 minutes on each side until partially cooked, then transfer to an oven-proof dish.

2 In the meantime, heat the vegetable oil in a frying pan. Fry the onions and garlic, stirring occasionally until tender. Stir in the curry powder, dried lime or lemon rind and salt.

3 Dissolve the tamarind paste in the warm water and add it to the onion mixture. Cook over a medium heat for 25 minutes, until it becomes a thick paste. Add the parsley and coriander.

4 Preheat the oven to 200° C / 400° F. Spread the onion mixture over the grilled fish. Cook in the oven for 15 to 20 minutes until the fish is cooked. Then place the fish under the grill for 1 minute until a thin crust has formed on the stuffing. Serve hot with a green salad.

EGYPT

SERVES 5

1 kg / 2 lb 3 oz white fish fillet, such as
  hamour or cod
1.5 litres / 3.2 pints (6^1/$_4$ cups) water
1 tsp salt
500 g /1 lb 2 oz potatoes, peeled and
  kept whole
2 garlic cloves, peeled and chopped
5 Tbsp fresh coriander, chopped
1 tsp black pepper
5 Tbsp parsley, chopped
^{1}/$_2$ tsp cinnamon
1 medium onion, peeled and finely chopped
1 beaten egg
40 g / 1^1/$_2$ oz (^{1}/$_4$ cup) breadcrumbs
3 Tbsp vegetable oil
Salad, bread or boiled rice, to serve
Wedge of lemon, to garnish

Kofta al samak
Minced fish

1 Place the fish in a saucepan. Add the water and salt and bring to the boil. Reduce the heat and poach the fish gently for 15 minutes. When cooked, gently remove the fish with a slotted spoon and reserve the liquid. Cook the potatoes in the fish water for 15 minutes.

2 Mince the fish and the boiled potatoes using a fork or a food processor. Add the garlic, coriander, pepper, parsley, cinnamon and onions and mix thoroughly. Divide the resulting paste into 30 balls the size of a small egg. Flatten them into patties and dip in the beaten egg, then coat with breadcrumbs.

3 Fry the fish patties in the hot vegetable oil until brown on both sides. Serve hot with a salad and bread or boiled white rice. Garnish with a wedge of lemon.

 BAHRAIN

SERVES 4–5

For the fish
1 kg /2 lb 3 oz hamour or 12 red mullet
1 Tbsp plain flour
2 Tbsp lemon juice
1 Tbsp salt
240 ml / 8 fl oz (1 cup) vegetable oil,
  for deep frying

For the marinade
1 Tbsp fresh coriander, chopped
125 ml / 4 fl oz (^{1}/$_2$ cup) white wine vinegar
1 tsp white pepper
^{1}/$_2$ tsp cinnamon
1 tsp cumin

Parsley sprigs, to garnish
1 lemon, cut into wedged, to garnish

Samak mishwi bil asiakh
Fish on skewers

1 Rinse the fish and pat it dry with paper towels. Rub it with the flour, lemon and salt.

2 To make the marinade, mix all the marinade ingredients together in a bowl. Add the fish and toss gently to coat. Cover and marinate for about 2 hours in the refrigerator.

3 Thread the whole fish onto bamboo skewers. Heat the vegetable oil in a frying pan and deep fry the fish for 6 to 7 minutes on both sides until golden brown. Remove and drain on absorbent paper.

4 Transfer the fish onto a serving dish. Serve with fried potato rings and toasted bread, and garnish with parsley sprigs and lemon wedges.

YEMEN

Sanouna
Hamour fish cutlets

SERVES 4–5

1 kg / 2 lb 3 oz whole hamour, or seabass,
  halibut or cod, cleaned and cut into cutlets
1/2 tsp of each: cumin, coriander, black
  pepper, cinnamon and turmeric
Salt, to taste
500 g / 1 lb 2 oz (2 1/2 cups) basmati
  or long grain rice
1 litre / 35 fl oz (4 cups) hot water
3 Tbsp vegetable oil
2 medium onions, peeled and thinly sliced
2 garlic cloves, peeled and crushed

1 Season the fish cutlets with all the spices and salt. Cover and refrigerate for 30 minutes.

2 Place the rice and water in a pan and bring to the boil. Cook over a medium heat for 10 minutes until the water has been absorbed and the rice is half cooked. Set aside.

3 Heat the vegetable oil in a frying pan. Fry the fish cutlets until golden brown on both sides. Remove from the heat and set aside. In the same pan, stir in the onions and cook over a medium heat for 5 minutes until golden brown. Add the garlic, stirring for 2 minutes.

4 Place half the quantity of cooked rice over the onions and top with the fish cutlets, then cover with the remaining rice. Sprinkle the rice with a little water, cover and simmer gently for 20 minutes until tender. Transfer the rice onto a large serving dish and place the fish on top. Serve hot.

KUWAIT

SERVES 4–5

300 g / 10¹/2 oz (1¹/2 cups) lentils
1 litre / 35 fl oz (4 cups) water
3 Tbsp vegetable oil
2 medium onions, peeled and chopped
2–3 garlic cloves, peeled and crushed
1 kg / 2 lb 3 oz raw prawns, shelled and
   deveined
1 tsp dried lime or lemon peel
Pinch of black pepper
Pinch of turmeric
Pinch of cardamom
5 cloves
90 g / 3 oz (1 cup) fresh coriander, chopped
400 g / 14 oz (2 cups) long grain rice, rinsed
Salt, to taste
Lemon slices, to garnish

Marbeen

Prawns with lentils and rice

1 Rinse the lentils and place them in a saucepan with the water. Bring to the boil and cook over a moderate heat for 20 minutes.

2 Heat the vegetable oil in a frying pan and add half the onion quantity. Cook until golden brown, then add the garlic, stirring for 2 minutes.

3 Add half the prawns, dried lime or lemon peel, pepper, turmeric, cardamom and cloves to the onions, stirring for 5 minutes. Stir in half the coriander, cover and simmer over a low heat for 5 minutes, until tender.

4 Add the prawn mixture to the lentils, then add the rice. Adjust the water quantity as needed to cover the rice and lentil mixture. Simmer over low a heat for about 30 minutes until the lentils and rice are tender and the sauce has thickened.

5 Fry the second half of prawns in vegetable oil for 3 minutes on each side. Add the remaining onion and coriander and season with salt and pepper. Cook for 3 minutes until tender, then remove from the heat and set aside.

6 Pour the lentil and rice mixture into a serving dish. Garnish with the fried prawns and lemon slices.

IRAN

SERVES 5–6

500 g / 1 lb 2 oz sole steaks
Pinch of salt
3 Tbsp vegetable oil
1/4 tsp turmeric
3 red peppers, deseeded and cubed
4 Tbsp fresh coriander, chopped
4 Tbsp parsley, chopped
2 Tbsp dill, chopped
1 large onion, peeled and chopped
6 cardamom pods
6 cloves
1 bay leaf
Black pepper, to taste
400 g / 14 oz (2 cups) basmati rice, rinsed
1 litre / 35 fl oz (4 cups) boiling water
Juice of 1 lemon
Fresh coriander, to garnish

Mohi polou
Sole steaks with herbed rice

1 Rinse the fish steaks, dry them with paper towels and sprinkle lightly with salt. Set aside for 20 minutes to absorb the salt.

2 Heat the vegetable oil in a pan and fry the fish steaks for 4 minutes on each side over a high heat. Transfer to a plate.

3 Add the turmeric, red peppers, coriander, parsley and dill to the pan and fry for 2 minutes, then lift from the pan.

4 Add the onion to the pan, stirring until golden brown. Add the cardamom pods, cloves, bay leaf and pepper, stirring for 1 minute, then add the rice and stir for 3 minutes. Season with salt.

5 Pour the boiling water over the rice and bring to the boil. Reduce the heat and simmer for 10 minutes, until half cooked. Remove half the quantity of rice from the pan and arrange the fish steaks on top of the rice in the pan. Sprinkle with the pepper mixture. Top with the remainder of the rice and lemon juice. Cover and simmer gently for 10 minutes. Transfer to a serving dish and serve hot, garnished with coriander.

DESSERTS

The following pages showcase a selection of delicious and simple-to-make sweet treats for any occasion. Ma'amoul (page 154), the semolina cakes stuffed with a nut filling are eaten to celebrate holidays. For festive occasions, why not try Baklawa (page 138), the filo pastry stuffed with nuts, or Atayef bil ashta (page 141), the thick pancakes oozing with a deliciously rich cottage cheese mixture topped with a sweet sugar syrup? Many of the desserts featured in the following pages are very simple and can be prepared in advance.

LEBANON

SERVES 4–6

1 Tbsp cornflour
3 Tbsp caster sugar
500 ml / 17 fl oz (2 cups) milk
1 gelatine leaf
1 tsp rose water
1 Tbsp orange flower water
60 g / 2 oz ($\frac{1}{3}$ cup) ground almonds,
  to garnish
60 g / 2 oz ($\frac{1}{3}$ cup) ground pistachio nuts,
  to garnish

KUWAIT

SERVES 8

200 g / 7 oz raisins
300 g / 10$\frac{1}{2}$ oz dried apricots
2 Tbsp clear runny honey
1 litre / 35 fl oz (4$\frac{1}{3}$ cups) water
1 tsp lemon juice
1 Tbsp rose water
1 Tbsp orange flower water
100 g / 3$\frac{1}{2}$ oz ($\frac{1}{2}$ cup) caster sugar
100 g / 3$\frac{1}{2}$ oz ($\frac{1}{2}$ cup) blanched almonds
100 g / 3$\frac{1}{2}$ oz ($\frac{1}{2}$ cup) pistachio nuts
100 g / 3$\frac{1}{2}$ oz ($\frac{1}{2}$ cup) pine nuts

Muhallabia
Milk pudding

1 Dissolve the cornflour, sugar and 60 ml / 2 fl oz ($\frac{1}{4}$ cup) of the milk in a heavy-based pan. Stir in the remaining milk and bring to the boil. Reduce the heat and simmer gently for 10 minutes, stirring constantly.

2 Add the gelatine leaf to the pan and simmer for a further 10 minutes. Then add the rose water and orange flower water, stirring for 1 minute. Remove from the heat and set aside until the mixture cools a little, then pour into a bowl. Cover and refrigerate for 3 or more hours. Turn the pudding onto a serving dish and garnish with almonds and pistachios.

Khoshaf
Dried fruits

1 Rinse the raisins and dried apricots and drain. Place them in a bowl with the honey and water. Cover and chill for 4 hours, then transfer to a serving bowl.

2 Dissolve the sugar in a little water. Stir in the lemon juice, rose water and orange flower water. Add to the dried fruits and toss to ensure that the fruits are coated in this mixture. Sprinkle with the nuts and serve cold with your choice of fruit juice.

 LEBANON

Aish al saraya
Sweet bread

SERVES 8

750 g / 1 lb 10 oz white bread, preferably
  unsalted
800 g / 1 lb 12 oz (4 cups) caster sugar
500 ml / 17 fl oz (2 cups) water
1 tsp lemon juice
1 Tbsp orange flower water
500 g / 1 lb 2 oz Ashta or ricotta cheese
200 ml / 7 fl oz (3/4 cup) double cream,
  whipped
200 g / 7 oz (1 cup) ground pistachio nuts

1 Remove the bread crusts with a sharp knife and discard. Toast the bread in a hot oven until lightly golden brown. Cool and break into very small pieces.

2 Place 200 g / 7 oz (1 cup) of the sugar in a saucepan and dissolve over a moderate heat, stirring constantly with a wooden spoon until golden brown. Add the water and the remaining sugar, stirring until dissolved. Leave over a moderate heat for 5 minutes without stirring.

3 Add the lemon juice and bread pieces to the pan. Stir for 3 minutes until the bread absorbs all the sugar syrup and becomes soft. Add the orange flower water and remove from the heat.

4 Pour the mixture in a large serving dish and crush any pieces that are still hard to a paste-like consistency. Flatten the surface with the back of a spoon and leave to cool.

5 In a bowl, mix the Ashta or ricotta cheese with the double cream. Spread evenly over the bread-syrup mixture, then sprinkle with a thick layer of pistachio nuts. Chill for 1 hour. Cut and serve.

IRAN

SERVES 4

325 g / 11¹/₂ oz butter
500 g / 1 lb 2 oz (3¹/₂ cups) plain flour
150 g / 5¹/₂ oz (³/₄ cup) caster sugar
1 tsp ground cinnamon
¹/₂ tsp cardamom
100 g / 3¹/₂ oz (1 cup) walnuts, halved
500 g / 1 lb 2 oz pitted dates
1 tsp ground pistachio nuts

Ranginak
Date fudge

1 Melt the butter over a medium heat in a heavy-based saucepan. Add the flour, stirring constantly, until golden brown. Remove from the heat and cool slightly. Add the sugar, cinnamon and cardamom to the flour and butter and mix well.

2 Pour half the flour mixture into a flat 25-cm (10-in) round dish and flatten the surface with the back of a spoon. Insert half a walnut inside each date and place the dates on top of the flour mixture. Cover the dates with the remaining flour mixture and again flatten the surface with the back of a spoon. Cut into diamond shapes. Sprinkle with ground pistachios and serve cold.

LEBANON

MAKES ABOUT 40 PIECES

For the pastry
500 g / 1 lb 2 oz (22 sheets) filo pastry
200 g / 7 oz unsalted butter, melted

For the nut filling
250 g / 9 oz (2 cups) coarsely ground
  almonds, walnuts or pine nuts
100 g / 3^1/$_2$ oz (^{1}/$_2$ cup) caster sugar
1 tsp orange flower water

For the sugar syrup
400 g / 14 oz (2 cups) caster sugar
375 ml / 12.6 fl oz (1^1/$_2$ cups) water
1 tsp lemon juice
2 tsp orange flower water

Baklawa

Filo stuffed with nuts

1 Allow the filo pastry to reach room temperature before using. Brush a large baking dish with a little melted butter. Trim the edges of the filo pastry to fit the size of the dish. Place a sheet of filo in the baking dish. Brush it with butter and top with another sheet, keeping the remainder covered with a damp towel. Repeat in the same manner until half (approximately 10) of the filo sheets are used.

2 Preheat the oven to 190° C / 375° F. To make the filling, combine the nuts with the sugar and orange flower water. Spread the nut filling over the filo sheets in the baking dish. Place a sheet of filo over the filling, brush with butter and repeat in the same manner until all sheets are used. Brush the top layer with butter and cut the layers into diamond shapes with a sharp knife. Bake for 1 hour until the top is lightly coloured. Drain any excess fat.

3 In the meantime, make the sugar syrup. Add the sugar and water to a saucepan, stirring over a medium heat until dissolved. Simmer for 15 minutes without stirring, then stir in the lemon juice and orange flower water just before removing from heat. When the syrup has cooled, pour it over the hot pastry and set aside to cool. Cut the pastry and store at room temperature in an air-tight container.

LEBANON

MAKES 16–18 PANCAKES

For the batter
1 tsp active dry yeast
1 tsp caster sugar
125 ml / 4 fl oz (1/2 cup) warm water
300 g / 10½ oz (2 cups) plain flour
Pinch of salt
375 ml / 12.6 fl oz (1½ cups) milk
60 g / 2 oz butter

For the filling
500 g / 1 lb 2 oz Ashta or cottage cheese
60 g / 2 oz (1/3 cup) ground pistachio nuts
2 Tbsp preserved orange blossoms

For the sugar syrup
400 g / 14½ oz (2 cups) caster sugar
375 ml / 12.6 fl oz (1½ cups) water
1 tsp lemon juice
2 tsp orange flower water

Atayef bil ashta
Pancakes with cream

1 Start by making the batter. In a mixing bowl, dissolve the yeast and sugar in the warm water. Sift the flour and salt into the bowl and gradually stir in the milk, beating until smooth. Cover the bowl and set aside to rest in a warm place for 1 hour until the batter has risen and doubled in size.

2 Heat a small heavy-based frying pan over a medium heat and grease very lightly with butter. Spoon the batter into a piping bag fitted with a round tip. Squeeze the batter in the pan and tilt immediately so that the batter spreads into a circle approximately 10 cm (4 in) in diameter. The pancake should be about 1/2 cm (1/4 inch) thick.

3 Cook for about 1 minute until golden brown on the underside. Flip over and cook for few seconds on the other side. Lift out and place on a plate, covering with a damp cloth to prevent drying. Repeat until all the batter has been used, stacking the pancakes one on top of the other.

4 Place 1 tablespoon of Ashta or cottage cheese on the pale side of the pancake. Fold over and press together half the edge, leaving the other half open with the Ashta protruding from it. Garnish with the ground pistachios and preserved orange blossoms.

5 To make the sugar syrup, add the sugar and water to a saucepan, stirring over a medium heat until dissolved. Simmer for 15 minutes without stirring, then stir in the lemon juice and orange flower water just before removing from heat. When the syrup has cooled, drizzle over the pancakes.

SAUDI ARABIA

SERVES 6–8

400 g / 14 oz (2 cups) caster sugar
250 ml / 9 fl oz (1 cup) water
1 tsp lemon juice
1 tsp cardamom powder
60 g / 2 oz (¹/3 cup) ground unsalted
   peanuts
300 g / 10¹/2 oz (3 cups) full cream
   milk powder

 SAUDI ARABIA

MAKES ABOUT 20 ROLLS

For the filling
300 g / 10¹/2 oz (1.5 cups) almonds or
   walnuts, finely ground
200 g / 7 oz (1 cup) caster sugar
1¹/2 tsp ground cardamom
Few saffron threads soaked in
   1 Tbsp rose water

For the pastry
16–20 sheets filo pastry
1 Tbsp cornflour
225 g / 8 oz (1 cup) ghee

Halawa labanieh
Cream and nut sweets

1 Place the sugar, water and lemon juice in a large saucepan. Cook over a low heat for 15 minutes until the syrup has thickened. Remove from the heat and set aside to cool.

2 Add the cardamom powder and ground peanuts to the syrup. Add half the milk powder, stirring well until blended. Gradually add the remaining milk powder, stirring thoroughly to obtain a smooth and consistent dough. Roll out the dough into small circles and arrange them on a serving dish. Serve with coffee.

Nashab
Fried nut rolls

1 Start by making the nut filling. In a bowl, combine all the filling ingredients together.

2 To prepare the pastry, cut the stacked sheets of filo pastry into 10 x 25-cm (4 x 10-in) strips. Cover with a damp towel to prevent them drying out.

3 In a bowl, dissolve the cornflour in 60 ml / 2 fl oz (¹/4 cup) water. Moisten the edges of the pastry with the cornflour water, then place 2 tablespoons of nut filling across the narrow end of the pastry strip. Fold the long sides of the pastry over the filling, pressing the folds along each side. Roll up firmly and press the edges to seal securely. Repeat with the remaining quantity.

4 Heat the ghee in a deep pan. Fry about five pastries at a time for 4 minutes, turning the rolls to brown them evenly. When the pastries are of a deep golden brown colour, remove and drain them on paper towels. Cool before serving. Store at room temperature in an air-tight container.

Cream and nut sweets

EGYPT

SERVES 6–8

For the batter
100 g / 3^1/$_2$ oz unsalted butter
150 g / 5^1/$_2$ oz (^{3}/$_4$ cup) caster sugar
1 tsp vanilla essence
2 medium eggs
350 g / 12^1/$_2$ oz (2 cups) semolina
1^1/$_2$ tsp baking powder
200 ml / 7 fl oz (^{3}/$_4$ cup) yoghurt
60 g / 2 oz (^{1}/$_2$ cup) blanched almonds

For the sugar syrup
475 ml / 16 fl oz (2 cups) water
400 g / 14 fl oz (2 cups) caster sugar
1 tsp lemon juice

Basbousa
Semolina cake

1 Preheat the oven to 190° C / 375° F. Start by making the batter. In a large bowl, beat the butter, sugar and vanilla until light and fluffy. Add the eggs and beat well. Gradually blend in the semolina and the baking powder. Add the yoghurt and mix well until the batter is smooth. Spread the batter into a greased 30-cm (12-in) round oven-proof pan. Cut into diamond shapes and place an almond in the centre of each diamond. Bake for about 35 minutes, until a knife inserted in centre comes out clean.

2 In the meantime, make the sugar syrup. In a saucepan, bring the water and sugar to the boil, then add the lemon juice and reduce the heat. Simmer, uncovered, for 10 minutes then remove from the heat and allow the syrup to cool.

3 When the cake is cooked, remove it from the oven and pour the cooled syrup over the hot cake. Cool, cut and store in an air-tight container.

IRAQ

SERVES 4

750 ml / 1^1/$_2$ pints (3 cups) water
100 g / 3^1/$_2$ oz (^{1}/$_2$ cup) caster sugar
60 g / 2 oz butter
90 g / 3 oz (^{1}/$_2$ cup) semolina
1 Tbsp rose water
1 Tbsp orange flower water
^{1}/$_2$ tsp ground cinnamon
1 Tbsp blanched almonds, to garnish

Mamounia
Semolina pudding

1 To make the sugar syrup, place the water and sugar in a saucepan and bring to the boil. Reduce the heat and simmer for 15 minutes. Set aside.

2 In a separate pan, melt the butter, then add the semolina, stirring constantly for about 5 minutes until golden brown. Stir in the sugar syrup and bring to the boil. Simmer over a low heat, stirring constantly until thickened. Remove from the heat, then add the rose water and orange flower water.

3 Pour into four serving dishes. Sprinkle with ground cinnamon and garnish with almonds.

Semolina pudding

LEBANON

MAKES 65 PIECES

For the dough

500 g / 1 lb 2 oz butter, softened at room
  temperature
600 g / 1 lb 5 oz (3 cups) caster sugar
600 g / 1 lb 5 oz (4 cups) plain flour, sieved
200 g / 7 oz (1 cup) pistachio nuts, chopped

For the filling

1 kg / 2 lb 3 oz dates, pitted and minced
45 g / 1¹/2 oz butter
45 g / 1¹/2 oz (¹/4 cup) caster sugar
2 Tbsp rose water

Tamara

Shortbread with dates

1 Start by making the dough. Place the butter in a mixing bowl and whisk on full speed with an electric mixer until light and fluffy. Gradually add the sugar, beating until light and creamy. Gradually fold in the flour, whisking the mixture until smooth. Cover the dough and leave to rest in a cool place for 1 hour.

2 To make the filling, combine the dates with the butter, sugar and rose water.

3 Preheat the oven to 190° C / 375° F. Divide the dough into walnut-size pieces. Flatten each piece with your hand and place 1 tablespoon of filling in the centre of each piece. Close and form into date shapes. Cover with pistachio nuts. Place on greased baking sheets.

4 Bake for 20 to 25 minutes until very lightly coloured. Do not overcook. Leave the shapes on the baking sheets to cool, then remove very carefully and serve or store in an air-tight container.

 BAHRAIN

SERVES 8

500 g / 1 lb 2 oz vermicelli
125 g / 4 oz butter
90 g / 3 oz (³/4 cup) ground almonds
200 ml / 7 fl oz (³/4 cup) condensed milk
¹/2 tsp vanilla essence
60 g / 2 oz (2 cups) cereal

Halwa al shairi wal laoz

Almond and vermicelli pastries

1 In a saucepan, fry the vermicelli in the butter until browned. Remove from the butter and drain. Combine the vermicelli with the almonds, condensed milk, vanilla and half the cereal. Mix well and set aside to cool. Shape the mixture into walnut-size balls and arrange them on a serving dish. Garnish with the remaining cereal.

SYRIA

Barazik
Sesame cookies

MAKES 50 COOKIES

For the sugar syrup
125 ml / 4 fl oz (^{1}/2 cup) water
200 g / 7 oz (1 cup) caster sugar
1 tsp lemon juice
Few drops of rose water or orange
  flower water

For the dough
250 g / 9 oz butter
300 g / 10^1/2 oz (1^1/2 cups) caster sugar
450 g / 1 lb (3 cups) plain flour
1 tbsp active dry yeast
250 ml / 9 fl oz (1 cup) milk
250 g / 9 oz (2^1/2 cups) sesame seeds
1 Tbsp butter, melted
150 g / 5^1/2 oz (^{3}/4 cup) pistachio nuts,
  chopped

1 Start by making the sugar syrup. Place the water and sugar in a small pan and bring to the boil. Simmer for about 10 minutes over a moderate heat until the syrup starts to thicken. Add the lemon juice and rose or orange flower water, then remove from the heat and set aside to cool.

2 To make the dough, whisk the butter with the sugar in a medium bowl until smooth. Stir in the flour, yeast and milk, beating constantly until smooth. Leave to rest for 15 minutes.

3 Preheat the oven to 190° C / 375° F. Mix the sesame seeds with the melted butter and sugar syrup. Divide the dough into large walnut-size balls. Flatten the balls with your fingers into 8-cm (3-in) flat circles. Coat one side with the sesame mixture and the other side with the chopped pistachios. Place the cookies onto ungreased baking trays and bake for 10 minutes until golden brown. Cool and store in an air-tight container.

EGYPT

SERVES 6

350 g / 12^1/2 oz puff pastry
1 litre / 35 fl oz (4^1/3 cups) milk
300 ml / 10^1/2 fl oz (1^1/4 cups) double cream
100 g / 3^1/2 oz (^{1}/2 cup) caster sugar
90 g / 3 oz (^{1}/2 cup) raisins
60 g / 2 oz (^{1}/3 cup) pistachio nuts
60 g / 2 oz (^{1}/3 cup) blanched almonds,
  slivered
60 g / 2 oz (^{1}/3 cup) pine nuts or
  chopped hazelnuts

Um ali
Cream and nut pastry

1 Preheat the oven to 190° C / 375° F. Roll out the pastry to fit a 30 x 20-cm (12 x 8-in) oven-proof dish. Bake for 10 minutes, until crisp and lightly coloured. When cool enough to handle, crush the pastry into medium-size pieces.

2 Combine the milk, cream and sugar in a heavy-based pan and bring to the boil. Reduce the heat and simmer gently for 5 minutes. Leave to cool.

3 In a bowl, mix the pastry pieces with the raisins and nuts. Pour the milk mixture over pastry mixture and leave to soak for 30 minutes. Bake in the oven for 20 minutes until golden brown. Serve hot.

 IRAN

MAKES 25 PIECES

200 g / 7 oz (1 cup) caster sugar
3 Tbsp clear runny honey
4 Tbsp corn oil
90 g / 3 oz (^{3}/4 cup) slivered almonds
^{1}/2 tsp ground saffron dissolved in
  2 Tbsp rose water
4 Tbsp chopped pistachio nuts, to garnish

Shohan asali
Honey almonds

1 Place the sugar, honey and corn oil in a heavy-based saucepan. Cook over a medium heat, stirring frequently until the sugar is melted and turns golden brown. Add the almonds to the pan and cook for about 2 to 3 minutes, until the almonds are coated.

2 Add the saffron-rose water and cook for 2 minutes, stirring occasionally. Make sure the mixture does not become too dark. Immediately pour teaspoonfuls of the mixture onto an aluminium foil-covered baking tray, leaving some space between each. Garnish with chopped pistachios. Allow the honey almonds to cool, then remove and arrange on a serving platter or keep in an air-tight container or biscuit jar.

50 g

SAUDI ARABIA

SERVES 5

For the milk pudding
250 ml / 9 fl oz (2 cups) milk
3 Tbsp cornflour
75 ml / 3 fl oz ($^1/_3$ cup) water
50 g / 2 oz ($^1/_4$ cup) caster sugar
2 tsp rose water

For the mango layer
500 ml / 17 fl oz (2 cups) mango juice
3 Tbsp cornflour
75 ml / 3 fl oz ($^1/_3$ cup) water
50 g / 2 oz ($^1/_4$ cup) caster sugar
Whipped cream (optional), to garnish
3 Tbsp ground pistachio nuts, to garnish

Muhallabia bil mango
Mango pudding

1 Start by making the milk pudding. Place the milk in a heavy-based saucepan. In a bowl, dissolve the cornflour in the water and add to the milk. Bring to the boil, reduce the heat and simmer gently for 15 minutes, until the mixture starts to thicken. Add the sugar and rose water and simmer for a further 5 minutes, stirring frequently. Remove from the heat and set aside.

2 To make the mango layer, place the mango juice in a saucepan. In a bowl, dissolve the cornflour in the water and add to the mango juice. Bring to the boil, reduce the heat and simmer gently for 15 minutes, until the mixture starts to thicken. Add the sugar and simmer for a further 5 minutes, stirring frequently. Remove from the heat.

3 Half fill five serving bowls with the milk pudding. Top with the mango syrup and garnish with whipped cream, if using, and sprinkle with ground pistachios.

LEBANON

MAKES 35–40 CAKES

For the dough
750 g / 1 lb 10 oz semolina
375 g / 13 oz butter
1 tsp active dry yeast
4 Tbsp warm water
60 ml / 2 fl oz (¹/4 cup) rose water
60 ml / 2 fl oz (¹/4 cup) orange flower water

For the fillings
250 g / 9 oz (2 cups) coarsely ground
  walnuts
400 g / 14 oz (2 cups) caster sugar
4 Tbsp rose water
4 Tbsp orange flower water
250 g / 9 oz (2 cups) coarsely ground
  blanched almonds
2 decorated moulds: 7.5 cm (3 in) for the
  almond cakes and 5-cm (2-in) round for
  the walnut cakes
200 g / 7 oz (1 cup) icing sugar, to dust

Ma'amoul
Semolina cakes

1 Start by making the dough. Place the semolina in a large bowl. Melt the butter over a low heat and pour it over the semolina. Mix until the butter is fully amalgamated. Cover and leave at room temperature overnight.

2 Dissolve the yeast in the warm water, then add it to the semolina mix. In separate pans, heat the rose water and orange flower water until hot then pour over the semolina. Mix with your hands to obtain a smooth dough.

3 Using a food processor, process the semolina mixture in four batches to a malleable dough, then knead the dough lightly with your hands. Place in a bowl, cover with a damp towel and leave to rest for 1 hour at room temperature.

4 To make the walnut filling, mix the walnuts with half the quantity of sugar, 2 tablespoons of rose water and 2 tablespoons of orange flower water. Make the almond filling by mixing the almonds with the remaining sugar, 2 tablespoons of rose water and 2 tablespoons of orange flower water.

5 Moisten your hands, then take a piece of dough the size of a large walnut and roll it into a ball. Make a large hole in the ball with your forefinger and squeeze in 2 tablespoons of either nut filling. Close and roll into a ball again.

6 Preheat the oven to 200° C / 400° F. Press the filled ball into one of the decorated moulds, then tap out onto a board. Place the shape on an ungreased baking tray. Repeat with the remaining balls, using one mould for the walnut-filled pastries and the other for the almond-filled pastries.

7 Bake for 10 minutes until slightly coloured. Remove from the oven and leave to cool on the tray for 3 minutes. Very carefully lift the cakes off the tray, taking care not to break them as the cakes are still soft. Place on trays lined with paper towels. Dust with a generous amount of icing sugar and leave to cool. Store in an air-tight container at room temperature.

KUWAIT

MAKES 30–35 PIECES

200 g / 7 oz clarified butter
200 g / 7 oz (1 cup) caster sugar
300 g / 10^1/$_2$ oz (2 cups) plain flour, sifted
60 g / 2 oz (^{1}/$_3$ cup) almonds, blanched
  and peeled

Ghraybeh

Shortbread

1 Place the clarified butter in a mixing bowl and beat on full speed of electric mixer until light and fluffy. Gradually add the sugar, beating until smooth and creamy.

2 Fold in the flour until well blended. Cover the dough and leave to rest in a cool place for 1 hour.

3 Preheat the oven to 150° C / 300° F. Shape the dough into walnut-size balls. Place them on ungreased baking trays. Press the centre of each piece gently with your fingers and place an almond in each indentation.

4 Bake for 20 to 25 minutes until very lightly coloured. Do not overcook. Leave to cool on the baking trays. Remove very carefully and store in an air-tight container.

UNITED ARAB EMIRATES

SERVES 6–8

125 ml / 4 fl oz (^{1}/2 cup) corn oil
175 g / 6 oz (1 cup) semolina
250 ml / 9 fl oz (1 cup) water
700 g / 1 lb 9 oz (2 cups) minced dates
1 tsp ground ginger
1 tsp ground cardamom
3 Tbsp blanched almonds, to garnish
3 Tbsp ground pistachio nuts, to garnish
Icing sugar, to dust

 LEBANON

MAKES TWO 1-LITRE (35-FL OZ) JARS

1 kg / 2 lb 3 oz yellow dates
2 litres / 70 fl oz (8 cups) water
60 g / 2 oz (^{1}/3 cup) blanched almonds
500 g / 1 lb 2 oz (2^1/2 cups) caster sugar
Peel of 1 mandarin or orange
8 cloves
Juice of ^{1}/2 lemon

Smid bi tamer
Semolina with dates

1 Heat the corn oil in a pan. Add the semolina and stir until lightly browned. Add the water and stir until all the liquid has been absorbed. Remove from the heat when the semolina starts sticking to bottom of pan. Add the dates, ginger and cardamom, stirring vigorously until well combined.

2 Pour the date mixture into a large well-greased serving dish and flatten with the back of a spoon. Garnish with the nuts and dust with icing sugar. Cut into squares and serve.

Murabba al balah
Preserved dates

1 Wash and peel the dates. Place them in a stainless steel pan, cover with the water and bring to the boil. Cook over a moderate heat for 30 minutes until tender. Remove from the water, drain and leave to cool in a colander. Reserve the cooking liquid.

2 Remove the pits from the dates, pushing them out with a cocktail stick or a pointed knife. Fill each date with a whole almond. Place the stuffed dates in a stainless steel pan, sprinkle with the sugar, orange peel, cloves and 375 ml / 12.6 fl oz (1^1/2 cups) of the reserved liquid. Soak for 12 hours.

3 Remove the dates from the sugar and water mixture and set aside. Pour the sugar and water into a stainless steel pan, bring to the boil for 5 minutes, skimming any froth as necessary. Add the dates and lemon juice to the pan and simmer for about 20 minutes, until the syrup thickens. Remove from the heat and pour into two 1-litre (35-fl oz) sterilized jars. Leave to cool before tightly closing the jars.

Glossary

Burghul

Cucumber

Dried limes

Freek

Allspice also known as pimento or Jamaican pepper. Available whole or ground. Tastes like a blend of cinnamon, cloves and nutmeg.

Ashta a thick cream widely used in pastries and sweets. Can be substituted with a mix of $3/4$ ricotta or cottage cheese to $1/4$ whipped double cream or mascarpone cheese.

Baharat mixed spices used in the Gulf countries and in Iraq. Baharat can be prepared by mixing the following spices: $1/3$ tsp black pepper, $1/4$ tsp dried coriander, $1/4$ tsp cinnamon, $1/4$ tsp cloves, $1/3$ tsp ground cumin, 2 tsp cardamom, $1/4$ tsp nutmeg, $1/2$ tsp paprika, $1/4$ tsp dried limes and $1/4$ tsp curry powder.

Basmati rice a slim and long grain rice with an aromatic flavour. The grains stay firm and separate during cooking. Rinse several times before cooking.

Blanched almonds almonds with skins removed. To blanch almonds, soak them in boiled water for 15 minutes. Drain, then press them with your fingers to remove the skins.

Broad beans see Fava beans.

Burghul (cracked wheat) wheat which is hulled, boiled, dried and ground into fine or coarse grains. It is a basic ingredient in Lebanese and Syrian cuisines.

Cardamom available in pods, seeds or powder. It is preferable to buy the pods as the seeds can be removed and used when needed. It has a distinctive aromatic flavour and is one of the world's most expensive spices.

Chickpeas an irregularly round, sand-coloured legume used extensively in Mediterranean cooking. Can be purchased canned or dried.

Chillies come in many types and sizes, both fresh and dried. Use rubber gloves when deseeding and chopping fresh chillies as they can burn the skin. Removing seeds and membranes reduces the heat level.

Cloves dried flower buds of a tropical tree native to Moluccas but also grown in other regions. The buds, stalks and leaves all yield aromatic oil of clove. Cloves are available whole or ground.

Coriander a strongly flavoured herb, also known as cilantro and Chinese parsley. Its seeds are the main ingredient of curry powder. Available fresh, ground and in seed form. Often stirred into a dish just before serving for maximum impact.

Cucumber the variety used in this book is the long, slender and thin-skinned Lebanese cucumber, also known as the European or burbles cucumber.

Cumin a spice with a strong and distinctive aroma. Available in seeds or ground.

Dried lime or loomi small, brown or black dried limes. Used frequently in Gulf cooking as well as in Iraq and Iran to impart a lemony flavour. After cooking, remove and discard the limes.

Fava beans used fresh and dried. The fresh bean, when young, has the same shape as green beans and is cooked in the same way. The dried bean is available precooked.

Filo pastry a very thin pastry used for making sweet and savoury dishes. Available fresh, chilled or frozen.

Freek wheat that is picked while still green and then toasted, hulled and dried.

Ghee (samneh) clarified butter with milk solids removed, so that it will not burn during cooking.

Green onion see Spring onion.

Hamour fish a fat-fleshed grouper fish found in the Gulf region. Can be substituted with cod or rockfish.

Hawail can be prepared by mixing the following spices: 3 tsp black pepper, $1^{1}/2$ tsp caraway, $1/2$ tsp ground saffron, $1/2$ tsp cardamom, 1 tsp turmeric.

Rose buds

Saffron strands

Tamarind

Orange flower water fragrant water extracted by distillation from orange blossoms. It is mainly used in Middle-Eastern cuisine to gently flavour sugar syrup and sweets. It is also used as a digestive. Available in Middle-Eastern, Greek and Turkish food shops. Always buy the natural variety.

Parsley parsley used in Middle Eastern cooking is of the flat-leaf variety also known as continental parsley.

Pine nuts also known as pignoli. These small, cream-coloured kernels are obtained from the cones of pine trees native to the Mediterranean region. They have a nutty flavour and are commonly used in stuffings and sweets and to garnish meat, chicken and fish dishes.

Pistachio nuts small, green nuts used unsalted to garnish savoury meat and chicken dishes as well as in desserts.

Pitta bread or pocket bread most widely used bread in the Middle East. This wheat-flour pocket bread is sold in large, flat pieces that separate easily into two thin circular pieces. Available in supermarkets and in Middle-Eastern food stores.

Pomegranate a warm-climate fruit about the size of a large orange, with leathery red skin and a myriad white seeds enveloped in its juicy pink flesh.

Pomegranate molasses reddish-brown sour syrup prepared from sour pomegranate fruit juice.

Purslane a green vegetable with small, fleshy leaves used in salads in the Lebanon and Syria. If unavailable, watercress may be used instead.

Rose water extracted by distillation from a very fragrant pink rose. It is mainly used in Middle-Eastern cuisine to flavour some meat dishes, sugar syrup, and in sweets. Always buy the natural variety.

Saffron available in strands or powder. It imparts a yellow-orange colour to food once infused. The quality varies greatly; the best is the most expensive spice in the world. If sealed properly, it can be stored in the freezer for up to one year.

Scallion *see* Spring onion.

Semolina also known as sooji. Used in puddings and sweets, it is made from durum wheat milled into various textured granules.

Spring onion also known as green onion or scallion. An immature onion picked before the bulb has fully formed, it has a long, bright green edible stalk and bulb.

Sumac the dried berries of a shrub that grows wild in the Mediterranean. The berries are ground into a reddish-purple powder. Imparts a sour flavour to salads and other food.

Tahini a thick, buttery fluid made from ground toasted sesame seeds.

Tamarind or Indian date the long, brown pods of a tropical tree with a strongly acidic taste. The dried pods are compressed and packaged like dates. To use, the required quantity is soaked and strained to separate the pulp from the sticky fibres and seeds.

Taro a large, starchy tuber with a dry-textured flesh and a flavour similar to potato. Bitter when eaten raw. Peel before using but protect hands with rubber gloves because its skin has tiny prickly fibres.

Thyme mix (zaatar) a mix containing dried thyme, sesame seeds, sumac and salt.

Tomato paste a concentrated tomato purée used to flavour soups, stews, sauces and casseroles, etc.

Turmeric a member of the ginger family. Its root is dried and ground, resulting in a rich yellow powder that is used in small quantities to colour rice, butter, cheese and mustard. Store in an air-tight container.

Vine leaves grapevine leaves are sold canned, fresh or preserved in brine. If using preserved vine leaves, rinse them thoroughly before use to remove the salty flavour, then soak in boiling water for 10 minutes to make pliable. Fresh vine leaves may be frozen in sealed plastic bags.

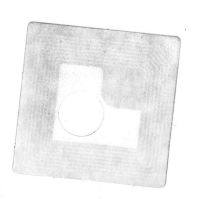